Mixed Frequencies:
New & Selected Poems

Peter Michelson

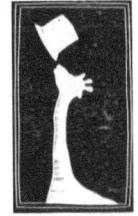

MadHat Press
Cheshire, Massachusetts

MadHat Press
PO Box 422, Cheshire MA 01225

Copyright © 2020 Peter Michelson
All rights reserved

The Library of Congress has assigned this edition a Control Number of 2019933018

ISBN 978-1-941196-86-1 (paperback)

Cover art and design by Marc Vincenz
Book design by MadHat Press
Author photo by Jake Rubinstein

www.madhat-press.com

First Printing

For Judith, the Priestess of the Dreams

*And for John and for Michael—Confrères ...
Eternally Durable ...*

Other Books by Peter Michelson

The Eater (poetry)

The Aesthetics of Pornography (criticism)

Pacific Plainsong I–XIII (poetry)

When the Revolution Really (poetry)

Speaking the Unspeakable (criticism)

The Extant Poetry and Prose of Max Michelson (as editor)

Preface

There have been three significant efforts to deal with the American West in contemporary poetry: Thomas McGrath's *Letter to an Imaginary Friend,* Ed Dorn's *Gunslinger* and Peter Michelson's *Pacific Plainsong.* McGrath's take was autobiographical and often, given his politics, global ("North Dakota is everywhere"). *Gunslinger,* a mock heroic epic, is at once comic, historical, contemporary and political. Both Dorn's early collection, *Geography,* and the later *Recollections of Gran Apacheria* also engage the matter of the West. *Pacific Plainsong,* begun at the same time Dorn was first composing *Gunslinger,* is unique in a number of ways. The attention is entirely on the treatment of Native Americans and the various rationalizations given to rape, mutilation, execution and high-minded extermination. The sequence returns to the Pacific Northwest of Michelson's youth through the medium of text, initially through the works of H.H. Bancroft, an eager 19th-century apologist for manifest destiny. Michelson's method is to recirculate Bancroft's and other texts within the more attentive and exacting space of the poem. It is a form of critical reading which exposes the intent of the texts and allows Michelson to recharge the language, to give it what he calls in one interview "a surge of language." This is public speech, sometimes synchronistic, often demotic, meant to confront, not just the notion of the American past, but its inherent sophistries, Poundian in its dependence on found materials but without Pound's deliberate fracturing. These are *songs,* after all, and *plainsongs* at that, monophonic with open rhythms.

    The first sections of *Pacific Plainsong* were published in 1967 and 1969. Their tonal reach, their "surge of language," characterizes much of Michelson's early poetry, represented here by the selection from *The Eater.* Peter is a big man, a college-football lineman, once considered by the New York Giants (his poem to Big Daddy Lipscomb is not collected here), so *The Eater* was, at once, a celebration of his size and self-deprecation. As a poetic persona, a voice for his poetry, *the eater* proposed a larger, more urgent sense of language, at times aggressively appetitive, as often, though, a comically outsized figure in the midst of an awkward dance or an unsuccessful seduction. The opening "Advertisement" is a clear indication that with this book in hand you're not, Toto, in the plain style of Kansas anymore. "Buy this book," it says, not books by Gary Snyder or Lawrence Ferlinghetti or the *Immortal Poems of the English Language,* which suffers from an excess of beauty. "Reader," he says, "we're Americans together," part of a dwindling group "Who love our mothers and who love our country." The promise is to "accentuate the positive" through a book meant to be read out loud with the family in front of the fire. "Advertisement" is perfect Michelson, an over-the-top satire of book sales pitches and a comic reproach to the modest, virtuous buckram of '50s establishment poetry. *The eater,* of course, betrays this huckster immediately, "Euclid be damned," he says, in response to an Edna St. Vincent Millay quote ("Euclid alone has looked on beauty bare"), "God damn his eunuch forms / I require shape for consummation, bare: / fruits have it...." This exclamation is the start of the poem's playfulness. Rhymes with "bare" ("pears," "flare," "fair," rare") and deft and comic quatrains emerge—

> so the eater
>   pursues his plan
>   assaulting shape
>   as best he can

And, of course, *the eater* means this as much as a statement of poetics as a menu, forms broken and replaced by more succulent forms. The appetite is for the volumes of archaic poetic gestures, provocative tones, rounded, organic, unrestrained and inherently performative--if not read with the family before the fire, then read out, certainly.

The opened form of "Whatever Happened to Rita Hayworth," one of Michelson's most celebrated early poems, works though a kind of serial structure, beginning with Rita in *Fire Down Below* with Jack Lemmon, who is pinned by a girder in the bilge of a burning tramp steamer, then spinning through other movies and marriages. "Whole armies have marched over me," Rita, as both love goddess and movie star, is equally victimized. Even *La Dolce Vita* is seen in passing, as is a parade of her varied Hollywood competition, a kind of cinematic Pindaric ode for the '50s. Its opposite is "The Eater, Impotent," as its title indicates, a failed sexual encounter, though lush in what it describes and in its language. always tempted, in tone and verse, into a lushly traditional romanticism, oddly, in *the eater's* bluntly described failure, a poetic success—

> … remembering
> the touch
> of mine upon her tongue, I left
> remembering, for still I drift and grope among the
> rumored graces of the young.

In mid-career Michelson traveled for extended stays to Finland, Sri Lanka and China. In poems from these ventures, the Eater's aggressive, appetitive stance and roiling language is replaced by the more narrative, less self-reflexive language of the witness. This is especially true of the Sri Lanka poems, which represent both the visitor's wonder at an exotic, tropic world and the explicit terrors of trying to negotiate a police state under siege by violent insurgents. The trick, Michelson says, after an extended encounter on the road with soldiers and their menacing machine guns, is not to get "between the ambusher and the ambushee." Taken into a Lankan home as both guest and witness, he meets a victim of a Tamil attack and is shown photos of the massacre. The scene is torturous, the poet caught between the victim and the photographs, with nowhere to turn—

> Meanwhile, we are, too like the Tigers, quick—
> our fragile witness borne
> upon those durable imperatives,
> grace and hospitality.

These four lines finely capture the dilemma of the witness, as quick to leave as the Tamil Tigers who committed the atrocity, he's there to bear witness, cradled for the moment, awkward as it is, in "grace and hospitality."

The poems from the Peoples' Republic of China are lighter in tone, narrative, as well, but deftly ironic. In an episode in a remote city, trying to deal with the Peoples Technological Cadre in charge of his inadequately plumbed and unheated apartment, Michelson quotes Chairman Mao to the leader of the group—"the theory of the radiator/ is coextensive with its practice.… / In theory *heat*, in practice, *heat.*" The technician simply

Peter Michelson

places his hand on the radiator and declares it fixed. China, in the wake of the Cultural Revolution is impenetrable, though for the poems quite engagingly so. If there is a kind of resolution to be had, it is to be found in the long poem about Chairman Mao as the potential poet-scholar turned political revolutionary dialectician and dictator, "The Chairman Premeditates his Yenan Talk on Literature and Art."

The China poems were first collected in the book, *When the Revolution Really*. There are two poems with that title. The Chinese version, called "Reconsidered," deals with the simple brutalities on a Chinese bus in the wake of "Four Modernizations and Several Courtesies Campaigns." The other, a Chicago poem, proposes a world in which the poet helps an old man get home safely and the passengers and driver on a CTA bus patiently wait, step by painful step, as an old woman slowly gets off the bus. The "revolution really" for Michelson—and this may be the lesson of both China and Sri Lanka—may be a matter of simple, quotidian care, as enduring, we might hope, as hospitality and grace. Michelson is at all times acutely aware of the politics in which his poetry operates, He manages the subtleties of Mao's operational aesthetics, the agilities required of re-educated writers and scholars, as well as the simple Red Book faith of the radiator technician, and his recourse to mutual support, patience and grace is earned, certainly.

This revolution is, however, an attractive, provisional fancy, quickly undone by our present politics, in "Homage to Malthus," the first of the group of New Poems that opens this collection, in which "the President wants to upstage Dr. Death" and the murderer, anti-hero of Mailer's *Executioner's Song*, Gary Gilmore, is a "model citizen." "The Chair" is a survey of chairness, objects of convenience and comfort but places where power sits, the chair we stand or even kneel before. Of course, the "extreme function" of the chair "we rightly call capital" is a place of execution and of a different civic pride. In a kind of poetic clemency, if not a legal one, the next poem speculates on waking and dreaming and poetic paradoxes within a suspended-animation, movie-like bar fight, a chair raised and held there at the poem's end. These recent poems engage once again the formal playfulness that was so much a part of the shocking originality of Michelson's first poems. There are variant villanelles here, a "Pantoum for William Cullen Bryant," quatrains that end with a rhyming triad, a truly lovely mid-winter poem whose self-consciously poetic diction seems as much a part of the celebration as food, dance and song.

Among the recent poems the richest is "The Priestess of the Dreams," dedicated to his long-time companion. In it the poet becomes the purveyor of her dreams, sometimes as the observer of her dreaming sleep, sometimes as the scribe of dreams recounted, experiences intimate and magical.

> What are the things
> that in the sentience of the night
>
> the priestess dreams?
> . . .
> The priestess dreams
> Of what we want to know—

The split iambic pentameter line here offering this intimacy a poetic certainty, one perfectly turned period among many in this sequence. The princess dreams the lucid light, its angles and dissonances, its factures at the Great Divide and its choreographies. In large measure her dreaming offers a kind of peace, though the days urgencies intrude— fatalities, abused labor, disease and suffering children. For the poet-skeptic, the irrepressible comedian, the princess dreamer is another, unique revolutionary. Gathering infants in her arms, she commandeers a train, just as her sleep commandeers music and reorders the light.

There has always been a calculated recklessness about Michelson's poetry, a wild surmise balanced by an acute sense of line and stanza, complex rhetorical periods and perfect, if unexpected, rhymes. For most of his career as a poet his stance has been bardic, his voicing deliberately public. In a recent interview with John Matthias for *Plume* Michelson said, "Liveliness has always been a factor in my work." His liveliness has had a broad reach—history and politics, aesthetics, pornography, art and the movies, life and death in Asia and in America, as well as, recently, a redemptive intimacy.

Table of Contents

Preface by Michael Anania vii

New Poems. Mixed Frequencies

I

Homage to Malthus	5
Of Monarchs and Hope	7
The Chair	10
Mixed Frequencies in the Golden West	11
The Day I Saw the Light	12
The Afflicted Man	13
Dithyramb Pythagorean	15
The Priestess of the Dreams	17
Pantoum for William Cullen Bryant	27
Bonjour Mon Amour Bonjour	29
New Year Skywatch	30
0 Degrees Centigrade	31
Betty Grable Digests the Lance of Rita's Dove	33

II

In Sad and Desperate Times	37
Memorial Virgilian, V. G.	38
As the Vernal Wood in Spring No Wedding Bower Blooms without a Song	39
Beginning in Finland	40
Recollecting Rubin	43
Heavy Metal	45
Song for Lucia	48
Midwinter Observance	50
A Recollection, Miraculous Jack's Melodious Knack	52
After the Fall	54

III

Chronicles of Ceylon	57
Milady Left Me Pizzicato	58
Colombo Airport	59
Rubber Match	61
We Like Americans	63
First Law of Lankan Dynamics	65
Setting Up Shop	66
Nature or Nurture	67
Pitching the Catch and Vice Versa	68
The Parable of Western Women and the Lankan Lizard	69
This a.m. in Batti Has Begun	70
Making Book	71
Bhikkhu Bashing, Six Bits	73
Mean Times Mean Demeanor	76
Official Habits	78
Talking at the Lakeview Inn	81
Wage-Slave Wages	83
Code of Road Behavior	84
Second Law of Lankan Dynamics	85
Enduring Witness, the Mosque at Kattankudi	86

Selected Poems. Plainsongs

from *The Eater* (1972)

Advertisement	93
The Eater	99
Going Hungry at Our Lady's Place	102
"It's cold …"	104

The Eater Goes 1) West, or 2) to the Movies	105
Whatever Happened to Rita Hayworth	108
Getting Hustled in a Laramie Bar	116
Hungry Eye at the Flin Flon	119
I Dream Profuse	122
The Eater, Impotent	124
Remembering May 4, 1970	133

from *When the Revolution Really* (1984)

I. Notes from the PRC

When the Revolution Really Reconsidered	139
Who Ever Doesn't Love the People	140
How Spring Comes to China	141
A Possibly Salutary Application of Chinese Jurisprudence	142
Dangling Conversation	143
The History of Lao Shui's Eyes	144
Míngtiān Means *Manaña*	146
Enroute to the Misty Peaks of Old Li Po	151
The Chairman Premeditates His Yenan Talks on Literature and Art	153

II. When the Revolution Really

When the Revolution Really	169
Parable for Our Time	173
Variations on Shooting an Elephant	175
Earth Air Fire Water and	177
Disarming	180
Contemplating the State of the Art	182

Peter Michelson

Our Children's Feasts	183
"All right, what"	186

from *Pacific Plainsong I–XIII* (1987)

I. Preface to *The Works* of H. H. Bancroft	191
II. "Today I met …"	196
III. Plainsong at Lapush	201
IV. Leschi's Mad Song	203
V. "Seattle is described …"	210
VII. Centenary Sequence for the Dreamers	217
XII. Chiricahua Plainsong	239
XIII. "Bestride the Mighty and Heretofore Deemed Endless Missouri"	250
Notes	269
Notes on the Poems	271
About the Author	275

New Poems
Mixed Frequencies

I

Homage to Malthus

Daniel Boone said it's time to move on
when you spot smoke on the horizon.
But today's news is
that some guy at the edge of town
had breakfast interrupted
by a cougar munching Fido
on his deck overlooking
what we now call *open space*.

Elsewhere, cattle ranchers learned
that grazing lands in national forests
are about to get gentrified
and doctors decline delivering babies
because malpractice insurance rates
are punching a hole through the ozone
and annual world rains increasingly provide
less than 1700 cubic meters of water per persona
and Albanians, Bosnians, Serbs, Sri Lankans
Rwandans & Sudanese
among a potpourri of others
are competing for the Third Reich's
ethnic cleansing record.

As if all that weren't enough
the President wants to upstage Dr. Death:
He urges us to "weed out questionable health-care costs"
by stipulating when we "should be allowed to die,"
the apparent assumption being
that redundant life encroaches
on liberty and the pursuit of happiness.
Remember Gary Gilmore, who knocked off

Peter Michelson

an innocent mechanic
then impatiently told
a malingering Utah firing squad
"Let's do it"?
These days, he's a model citizen.

Of Monarchs and Hope

for J and I

There is a laedie who speaks in season, Where
there is hope, she says it is said,
there is life. It is often said reverso.
Yet the truth is as she says it.
Come celebrate, she says, the triumph of hope.

Again is it even as she says.
Experience, which is its own reward,
is no obstacle. Hope is the thing
with wings, a fluttering lively thing that bounces
upon the air and flings itself to the winds,

always its delicate wings brilliant and buoyant
as sails before or athwart the breeze.
Beginning in the ever fickle northern chill
in Colorado or Saskatchewan or
Virginia, Dalmatia or Tashkent,

it will shed its skin perhaps four times,
facing predators, parasites, and opportunists,
surviving not on honeydew
nor on meringues of paradise
but on the milkweed thistle's nectar

before descending toward the highland tropics.
No creature else so slight and pending goes
thus far to find its portion, its only goal
by way of pheromones to lure to each
a lover to her side or his, "Their only

Peter Michelson

goal…," or so it's said. The trek's a trip …
along magnetic valences
of the Adirondacks, Great Plains, the Rockies,
the west Coast Range, the grand Pacific chasms—
always south by west, from south to southwest as

the origin of flight moves west to east,
toward convergence with the highland tropics
and a glinting in the eye.…
Celestially aligned, the sun's angle
on the horizon and the moon and stars

as well, they fly erratic but relentless,
each to the other sooner or later a polar
field in the alto plano forests,
at once umbrella and comforter, of those
Transvolcanic cordilleras. There,

"After nearly 14 years traversing
continents, scaling mountains, walking
ancient trails, exploring seas, marrying,
divorcing, enduring wars, insurgencies,
the U.N. & other chaos" they pause, each

before the other, the laedie who speaks in season
and her beloved wayfarer, they pause
in a shock of recognition, in acceptance of
their improvisational lives, their years
traversing continents, they pause in cognizance—

she of his bright durance amid travails,
he of her lucid beauty amid travails—
and still does experience after all
fare well with them, as even from its wreckage
does the excellence of their love emerge.

Peter Michelson

The Chair

is genderless, generous we hope
and sui generis, definitive
in ruling now & then unruly factions.
It's by and large a good position,
with provisos—one when in churlish times
it switches from the catbird to the hot seat,
and one when in parlous times
its disposition smacks of Nazis.
Notes the bard, uneasy rests
the seat that sits the throne, not least
because, though gilded, grand and gorgeously
embellished, its bottom line
is often architecturally severe.
Still, cushy, carved or careless of anatomy,
from recorded time we know
it's always been the sign and sentience of
authority—that apt coinage, the seat of power,
certainly requires the chair to sit it in.
And where it sits we stand before
or in extremis kneel in fealty, proposal,
and other servitudes. That's how it's always been.
But as we know, authority rhymes
with criminality, and we're Americans.
When the couplet gets more cozy than
our tolerance, our constitutional conventions
now suppose a tolerance for extreme function,
we rightly call it capital and wish
it weren't so rare.... Nonetheless, we're proud
we're free to sit selective culprits in the chair.

Mixed Frequencies in the Golden West

He lifts the chair above his head.
The sun sets red in the Golden west.
Brilliant planes of evening glare
from the crystal edge, and we
are in the poise of moves as yet unmade.
Questions rise like reasonable chairs
and hover with the menace in his eye.
The red end of the spectrum burns.
Things stretch farther than the eye can see.
What's the premise of receding light?
Later on in fact the barman, sobbing,
beat back the waves, sobbed
and beat them back with all his might.
Though poets wonder if they wake or dream
there are devices that convert
mixed frequencies to one incisive beam.
Some say oneiric terrors purge us,
Some prefer a fight.
The chair's incisively above us.
The agonist holds tight.

Peter Michelson

The Day I Saw the Light

for Frank Cunningham

was the day "Cute Pig"
had had enough.
He strode up the aisle
in his oxford button-down
and the only Ivy League tie
we had ever seen.
His tensed isosceles jaw annunciated
lucid vectors of intent
sharper than the stench of my dead meat
focused in his condor eye.
And his exquisite oarsman's hand
gripped a tome incisive as a stroke....
Which is all surmise—
I never, like a lot of things
before and since, saw it coming.
From the impact I would guess
volume four of *The Decline and Fall*.
In my surprise I saw auroras burst
more glorious and brutal than Caesar's reign,
more beyond reproach than Caesar's wife.
Forty years later I shook that same sure hand
and looked in that exacting eye.
I somehow didn't say what now I will,
that that old borealis is bursting still.

The Afflicted Man

Across the street bathed today
in the stunningly predictable pastels
each autumn brings lives the young
afflicted man. Ganglia withering
daily like a tree with falling sap
he brings things out.

Neighbors rake leaves, shovel snow, prepare
his meals. Cab drivers who for us
no longer even reach to flip
the handle on the door carry groceries
to his kitchen. Today a friend in red
arrives to take him for a drive.

He emerges to the brilliant morning chill.
His sallow forehead sports a bright
green band. His pants are flared.
He leans heavy on his metal cane, groping
for the shoulder of his friend. They descend
the stairs. His friend's pace is straight,

slow and steady; he reaches across
his chest like an old Roman in salute
to cover the afflicted man's unsteady hand
with his. They walk in halting cadence
to the car, a Mercedes convertible coupe
gleaming in the season's light. The afflicted

man lets go the shoulder. His hand
quakes toward the handle on the door.
He smiles ... make one move or even stoop

Peter Michelson

to gesture toward that door and my last act
before I sprawl into the street will be
to crack your knuckles with my cane....
His friend returns the smile, waits erect and still.

Dithyramb Pythagorean

One way or another there is
always may be necessarily
some thing or body else
the very being of the one
affirmed by reference to
the other where the one refers
to the one and the other to
the other one by which
we after all compute
the gravity of situations
mass divided by the square
of distance and so on it's
no secret these days that even
the sedentary chair's all atwitter
inside where it counts for
instance even sticks and stones
near or far like every body are
in proximity subject to twitter
and motion and every manner of
distraction from stick-&-stoneness
according as you know
to the gravity and so on and
every thing or body acts more
or less predictably depending
on mass distance disposition and
in some cases friction or
bodies in motion or at rest
(cf. atwitter inside, above) and
those who should know tell you that
for every action there is one
equally opposite which is how

Peter Michelson

those big blowups you hear so much
about these days occur so
there's a lot to consider but
according to the papers it's
mostly common knowledge now and
you can figure it out for yourself.

The Priestess of the Dreams

for J

1. She Dreams

the lucid light is grey. Pennants
flutter all the way from where
we were to where we started when
the sun was angled right.

She dreams her way
back home again. She tends the time,
the byways underground.
To the end of days

the priestess dreams....
She marks the way
to the yonder string band rendezvous
where the green girl climbs the ivied wall.

And mothers dance, their babies
bobbling on their bellies.
Hold your head on straight, she says.
The green girls climb.

They keep the time on toy guitars.
The priestess dreams.
The yonder string band claps.
All the babies clap their hands.

Peter Michelson

Are these the things that we'll remember
when all the catastrophic klezmer stops?
Where are the things
that in the sentience of the night

the priestess dreams?
The breeze wafts through madrona trees,
their leaves clacking by the sea.
The tides relentlessly are lapping,

remember? at the shore.
Half a million heartbeats race....
The priestess dreams
Of what we want to know—

the pace of things
the absent angle of the sun
the aurora's arc
the lucid bright grey light.

There in the park
are all the things we need
recall—the priestess tending time
babies bobbling on maternal bellies

the lurid smile at the end of days.
The green girl climbs.
Her shoes and dress are green
so green they fluff the elegies of night.

Where are the things we will remember?
They're in the park.
They're in the tides.
They're in the angle of the sun.

The yonder string band claps clap clap.
All the babies clap their hands.
The priestess dreams
the lucid light.

Her dreams anticipate
the counterpoints of sight,
all the way from where we started
to all the dissonance of night.

Peter Michelson

2. The Priestess Whistling

No question,
no question but it's dark
It's dark in darkest Africa where
We have never been
It's dark in the old cantons of China where
the lights are burning dim
It's dark we know in Petersburg
Tallinn and most especially D.C.
It's even dark in gay Paris

No question,
No question but everywhere it's dark
Still, you dream you dream and dream distraught
as only you can dream
And yet the light sometimes competes
as when you dream of infants crying
Their cries evolve to words
words as in their own beginning
And toddlers motion, "G'amma come!"

No question,
No question but it's dark
The dark surrounds the light you dream
Still, the light sometimes survives
Here I am
And you / whistling in the dark
Where the dream sometimes survives....
No question but we whistle, Love

No question but it's dark
Whistle, Love, breathe, in whistling we survive....

Peter Michelson

3. The Priestess Scans the News

We visit Belgium, Pittsburgh and possibly it's France,
And of the three Pittsburgh is your preference.
And it gets worse than that. Phantasms propagate....
The Cancun Warbucks went down in flames.
This year Rio must reach beyond the Greens
who cannot seem to reach the poor.
At Commodities Ltd, which is somewhere near,
it's 56 fatalities & tons of copper ore,
not to mention several billion dollars, yen or euro.
Meanwhile Muqtada al-Sadr calls off all attacks …
But homophobians strike the Middle East.
And Arabs buy up all the Arctic ice.
And a Japanese bobblehead declares, "About Chernobyl, who cares."
And right-wing warlocks attack New Orleans' abortion rights.
People are getting fired from here to Fond du Lac
and don't expect their paychecks coming back....
The warlocks steal the dreams of commonweal …
as the Priestess has said before … and will,
It ain't Kabuki, Babe, they're stealing it for real.
So here we are, she adds, amid malevolence
with no defense save love for one another.
Just love and this bu-ket of roses.
And, as for those, let me repeat,
the *fresca dulce* Rose alone is, like you my Love, replete.

4. The Lunar Light

The moon's full poise
glows crimson to and from
the peaks of the Great Divide
It is after all as if the sun
setting on the moon spreads
its blood orange flow across
the continent adrift in seas of time
The earth is bathed She sees the blood
of ages flood the continents adrift
The moon is bathed She sees the earth
encroach inconstant lunar latitudes
It deflects the light
The continents beneath the moon
shimmer blood orange Blood orange
peaks ... the Great Divide In fractured light
She sees this choreography of light this
pavanne this wonderous sight It's beautiful
she sighs It's beauty and she weeps
for all the history of obliterated light
Let, she thinks, the crimson night be blest ...
Let the moon pass on ...
Let the light devolve to shade ...
After all ... the seas of time ... Let there be some rest....

Peter Michelson

5. The News from Everywhere …

    "It ain't Kabuki Babe, they're losing it for real"

In her seventh decade
she dreams the agonistes of the age
that she's an antique
doll her face of porcelain but eyes
her eyes are all too real
Her ragged heart pumps plasma
plasma by the barrel
The price is right She sees it trickle down
"We are Americans
the patriotic people
The Civil War The Spanish War The World War
Korea Vietnam Granada"
Nada Nada It trickles down
The workers work It trickles down
The workers fast It trickles down
The great bell tolls

E. Coli walks the streets
muslims eating watermelon in the yard
Patriotic fervor fills the Fourth
Kim Jong Il invites the children in
Their eyes are huge and dark
The mosque explodes all hell erupts
Nada Nada It trickles down
"We're still at war"
Nada Nada It trickles down It trickles down
The great bell tolls

The Priestess gathers infants in her arms
"I saved hundreds but
what of those who died I think of that"
It trickles down
She commandeers a train
She fills the cars with children
She leads them through this world
At every checkpoint she declares
her orders from on high
You will not compute these ones
their calculus beyond your profit margin
In each hand a stone
A stone to place upon the bier
I think of that
It trickles down
The great bell tolls

"My drive is to revise Regression's Law"
Open the gates Install the orchid beds
the carousels with hyenas gaily lacquered
I think of that
the young one with the baleful eyes
innocent mustache and marginal IQ
He's out of work
and understandably annoyed
with the hungry child's squall
And slamming him in the manner of
rural women slapping
wet muslin against the stones
I think of that

Peter Michelson

It trickles down
The great bell tolls

"These are the sympathetic cases"
Nada Nada the Priestess says
Open up the gates
Install the orchid beds
the gaily lacquered carousel
the pools with golden carp
and blossoms bright above the lily pads
In the iris of her eyes the sight
of children slammed
in the manner of rural women
slapping wet muslin against the stones
Nada Nada the Priestess moans
She gathers infants in her arms
She commandeers a train
In the iris of her eyes the sight
I think of that
It trickles down
The great bell tolls

Pantoum for William Cullen Bryant

Not everybody rhapsodizes Bill
these days. He contemplated death too young.
It was a freight that solemn time bore well.
Still, he craved an antique spirit's tongue,

And though he contemplated death too young
it's to the point that he admired trees
while craving still an antique spirit's tongue.
He brought exotic fruits from overseas.

It's to the point that he admired trees,
configured in their groves a native hope.
Among exotic fruits from overseas,
Bartholdi's colossal Lady's colossal scope.

Configured in these groves of native hope
he heard the destined hum of multitudes
attending this colossal Lady's scope.
Her promise was pacific interludes.

He hymned the destiny of multitudes.
He saw it flooding from a cosmic urn—
the promise was pacific interludes.
But Black Hawk sensed more a mortal turn

in the cosmic hand that tipped the cosmic urn—
that is, a native thanatopsis
Black Hawk sensed, and not a comic turn …
The Bitch delivered on her promiscuous promise.

Peter Michelson

So it goes, the native thanatopsis....
Given the cosmic burn, what's so rare is
the Bitch delivered on her promiscuous promise.
So Bill rode horseback over Black Hawk's prairies.

Given comic turns, what's so rare is
that Bill inclined to call a horse a *steed*
and rode *airy undulations,* i.e. prairies,
but sat a saddle a hundred miles. Indeed,

he did incline to call a horse a steed
and fancied Mound Folk harnessed buffalo,
but he sat a saddle a hundred miles indeed.
Black Hawk went the way ancestors go.

Bill fancied Mound Folk harnessed buffalo,
It was freight that solemn time bore well.
Black Hawk went the way ancestors go....
Not everybody rhapsodizes Bill.

Bonjour Mon Amour Bonjour

for J

You my Rose my Opal my Gem *ma Perle*
My Jewel *mon Bijou mon plupart Fantastique de Fleurs*
It's such a pleasure to bid you *mon Éclair*
Mon Exotique ma Beauté to bid you *Bonjour*

To admire as you *coiffe* your *coiffure du jour*
And ogle your figure superb as the old *dependence en pierre*
Especially as you assemble your *très très jolie* brassiere
Such *plaisir ma Pierre Precieuse* to bid you *Bonjour*

Ah in your lovely *déshabillé* or *lingerie dangereuse*
I love you *mon Amour mon Bijou* exquisitely *précieuse*
And long let us live with *bonheur* and *la vie amoureuse*
Such pleasure *mon Amour* to bid you *Bonjour*

Peter Michelson

New Year Skywatch

This earth, our oasis amid
the galaxies … there
the lucent primordial vapors
bask in ultra violet shards
of failing solstice light.
Like us its energies are latent,
awaiting, say astronomers,
sensibility, sensible as an Indonesian
thunderhead floods an El Sonora wash.
This northern spiral turns against the clock.
The cycle inside accelerates
to gale force and more
and forms a central eye.
Now the energy's beyond compare.
It renders even ultimate arsenals obsolete.
Prodigious changes poise,
enough to heave ten million million
tons of water into the air.
Instantaneous evaporation.
However much we search we find no match.
It's latency's conversion to sensibility.
We're at the center … what is it that we watch?

0 Degrees Centigrade

lower these cans in the brine
fill them
when they're solid
hoist them with the winch
set them to season in the heat
until they slide out
like a 250-pound banana
from its skin.
Deftly with the pick
 break one down …

Later
climbing the stairway
I've got the leather
on my shoulder and
steadied with the tongs
the 30-pound cake atop it
I heft it into place

"Thank you Ice man," she says
Then, "Ice man, Take off yo' pants"
She's a solid no nonsense woman.
"Ice man," she says again
"Take off yo' pants"
"Yo' pants!" she says, pointing
like I'm maybe not too bright.
I look down   where she's pointing
The cloth is rent which is how she sees it
and how she says it

Peter Michelson

"Yo' *pants*," she says again pointing still
When she stands we're looking nearly eye to eye
She's a solid no-nonsense woman
I remove the garment of my shame

Betty Grable Digests the Lance of Rita's Dove

for K. B.

Finally it was an elegance
beyond her years arresting as

she later thought the moment of
her image so adroitly pinned

upon the cortex of the time's
precarious imperative.

Or perhaps it was the murmur
of its decay quiescent

as mortality picking pockets
beneath the aegis of the equinox.

Seven incisive epithets
teased the modulations of her memory

though they faltered on
the fulcrum of her tongue.

The whorl of her bejeweled digits
gestured four degrees northeast

Orion's celestial belt
an eloquence again beyond her years.

Her recall then was all she might
have wished had wishing been

Peter Michelson

her deviance. No not then or ever.
It was the pin as stainless as

the true madonna's honor.
Amongst so much she'd had to swallow that.

The question burned like Betelgeuse,
would she ever feel its prick again.

II

In Sad and Desperate Times

    for F and M

In the chiaroscuro of these times,
the "sad and desperate times" wherein we seek
felicities beyond the hope we prime,
we choose, when choose we can, the light. Fantastic

these "sad and desperate times," and so we seek
nearby or far "a tiny wild park"
and choose, when choose we can, to write fantastic
paeans to harmonize the light and dark.

Nearby or far "a tiny wild park"
informs the fecund wind with counterpoint,
a paean to harmonize the light and dark.
The lucid cadence rises to anoint

the fecund wind informed with counterpoint.
At summer's end the mountain Flora chance
a lucid cadence. Rising to anoint
the twining grasses, summer blossoms dance

at summer's end. The mountain Flora chance
their blossoms to the waning season's light.
Amid the twining grasses blossoms dance,
and we are blessed who stand to face the sight.

Such blossoms bring in that waning light
felicities bequeathed by love's bright prime.
And we are blessed who stand to face the sight,
that keen chiaroscuro of our time.

Peter Michelson

Memorial Virgilian, V. G.

His art was living—impudent audacious
rococo artless as a hall of mirrors

His last salon announced
a medium to outlast his eloquence

His affect then as nimble as his tanks
and tubes were sullenly impertinent

We toasted immortality
caroused for days and nights on end

Long past some midnight
as I took my leave the band played on

His anchoritic skull once nappy as a ram
disdained its morbid nasal tether

He inscribed among the constellations
a twist a boogaloo a buck and wing

He'd swat his raucous tambourine
strut incisive as a goat

God I never knew a man cashier mortality
quite so magisterially as that

As the Vernal Wood in Spring No Wedding Bower Blooms without a Song

for C & N

Astride the sanguine aegis of Mars, our Evening Star,
and before the benediction of the Morning Star,
these most articulate of all the stars,

we gather, witnesses to the logic of
as we are witness to the body of …
we gather, witness to the eloquence of Love.

Here in this high meadow's prescient air
comes now the bridegroom raising higher
than those sighing pines, yet but a share

of his devotion to, O happy groom
whom his own Aphrodite's brought to bloom
a bride so poised within the girdle of her charms.

So we witness now the timeless *Matrimonio*,
we hoist salutes with *Antipasto* and the *veritas* of *Vino*,
and then the lute, pretty-footed Terpsichore, and *Mangiamo!*

Ah tonight, tonight the groom will see his bride reflect the lucent moon,
and, yes, before the lustrous Pleiades and Mars go down
will Love, that loosener of limbs, inject his honeyed venom …

Above and all around we see the workings of …
O Lord we ask, O Lord of all you may be Lord of,
we ask Your blessing on this testament of Love.

Peter Michelson

Beginning in Finland

Here in Finland they say *Yatkuu Yatkuu*
Keep on truckin'
Yatkuu Yatkuu whatcha gonna do …
The news from everywhere is weird to bad
Yatkuu Yatkuu whatcha gonna do …
They're losing it in New York City
They're losing it in gay Paree
They're losing it in Kandahar
In Jaffna Islamabad Madrid
The news from everywhere's a gone bad deal
And the Priestess of the Dreams says
It ain't kabuki Babe, they're losing it for real …

But here in Turku here in the Buddha Bar
The Finns go boogie boogie
They boogie with the beat
The Finns got big black boots
Big black boots for big Finn feet
They're boogieing with Marilyn
They're boogieing with Mao
They're boogieing with Warhol
He's an honorary Finn
He boogies in his boots
Big black boots for his closet Finn feet
All the while the Buddha smiles
Everybody loves a dancing Finn

Suddenly the news from everywhere goes from bad to good …
The news is ringing through the world
The news runs up and down the Aura
Up and down the Seine

The news is on the Amazon, the Congo, the Mississippi and the Thames
The news is crossing Adam's Bridge
Riva and Rohan are getting married!

Say What?
Riva and Rohan are marrying!
The Finns are dancing as we speak
Winter's gone Summer is a solar feast
The news from everywhere is good
Peace breaks out in Lanka, i.e. Sri
The Taliban makes tapioca for Talmudic girls
Pakistanis come to Delhi for a pizza
The PRC tickles Taiwan's little feet
Swansdown swirls round Iraqi scimitars
Symphonic sweetmeats ride the borealis
Peace breaks out in Lanka, Sri
Riva and Rohan are marrying!

Who could guess
We all made bets
It's been so long I can't recall
Which way my money's down
But now whichever way it went I win
Riva and Rohan are marrying!
They've been practicing for years
They're perfect!
Oh Holy Happiness Happen Happily
Riva and Rohan are marrying!
The Smiling Buddha smiles
The Finns are dancing as we speak
The world's delirious throughout all seven seas

Peter Michelson

We drink an actual factual virtual and potent toast
And then we all envision *whirled peas!*

Yatkuu Yatkuu Keep on truckin'
Yatkuu Yatkuu It's the old New Deal
And the Priestess of the Dreams says,
It ain't kabuki Babe, they're marrying for real!

Recollecting Rubin from the Start

A New York City kid ecstatic at
the heady outwest mountainscape....
I took him for a natural enthusiast.

Our first words were sophistry
but not impertinent....
Life's a pile of shit, I said
apropos I can't remember what,
and women are the beetle on its peak.
He cocked an eye, looking like
an antic Ivan miming Eisenstein.
Take a couple Valium, he chortled,
we'll talk again next week.

I snorted when again he got ecstatic at
the postage stamp of land he'd bought,
as if a dickering in real estate
confirmed the faith of Canaanites.
Whatever was his salience
I took him for a Big Rock-Candy rhapsodist.

So we smiled our separate smiles
and went our separate ways
which now and then would cross.

Lately in the squalling season
with the water running high
I'd see him angling in the river.
He cast upstream against the flow.
His technique was vigorous

Peter Michelson

and I admired how his line
looped and caught the failing light.

But he could use
a bit more wrist, I thought,
and trusts too much the footing
on that tricky river rock.
Still, he was in the river
pitched against the run
and I was idle on the bank.

He cast again and hit a hole
where you knew some big ones lurked.
Then the surging river caught him
just as his line went tight,
perhaps a cutthroat or a walleyed pike.
His fist thrust up to play the line …
Whatever else he may have thought
as he went under
he knew he had a strike.

Heavy Metal, the Anniversary

for L and M

The first was frivolous though fine, a cotton cambric
lucid still among our fraying recollections …
But Gödel's Proof is truly poetry,
Where it is said, and rightly, that
"There's a helluva good universe next door!"
Let's go, you said, and did—

Tripping across the cosmos from stone
to precious stone—pearl, coral ruby, sapphire—
alighting now at this your fifth decade aflowering …

Amid the signifying violets here,
another rich deposit of the earth—
its symbol Au, its elemental number's up
aureate, ascending, an emanation, bright
circumference luminous as its atomic radius
spreads from kind to human kind …

Aurum, said the Romans, used
by early humanoids, gleaned
from the surface of the earth,
easily worked, beautiful and enduring …
discovered almost exclusively uncombined
excepting the telluridic Colorado ores,
as tiny flakes in quartz or among the shifting
streambed sands as well of course
as fabled rich high mountain veins.

Peter Michelson

Rich veins fabled
in the lore and lyred resonance of love
auspiciously abundant veins exquisite
and timeless among rare nuggets
heavier than a common man might heft.

Its *aural* state is malleable yet stable,
durable and universally admired,
lustrous though among the heaviest …
Rich and fabled, sought for love
As Psyche sought her Cupid
Cupiditas and bore Volupta to her breast …
So golden Apuleius whispers still
among the ancient fables …

Hellespont, Argonauts, chivalric codes …
Chivalrous, amenable, an excellent conductor
impervious to most malevolence,
gold succumbs alone to aqua regia
and cyanide, that uniformly lethal synthesis.
Thus, note well, this lovely metal alloys readily—
When its solutions are reduced
a colloid forms, pathologically miasmic—
a vapor much refrained throughout the lore of love—
and even 18 carats signify disease.
Hence the eloquence of gold
lies not in purity but in its ready alloy,
its configurations at the works of hands and days.

Therefore is leaf to airy thinness beat
much prized for its contrapuntal evocation

of frailty and long adorns cornice, incunabula,
canvas, photograph, plate and Sovereign Declaration.
So, if mortality be frail then durability
is transcendent, as are you extraordinary two,
cleaving together even as you promised
in your transcendent innocence
those five deranged decades ago.
The Golden Rose is a well-wrought work
and much adorned with beatitude and jewels,
but the sweet briar rose has what the gold has not,
and has what you who are so dear likewise do—
the wondrous fragrance and the frailty of life.

Peter Michelson

Song for Lucia

Lucia's come back to Colorado
The exquisite soul of Lucia's come back
the beautiful Señora's soul
the soul of the matchless words of Lucia
Lucia's come back to Colorado

She's brought the blossoms of Cinco de Mayo
She's brought the wishbones of her Andean doves
the metaphysical poppies of Machu Picchu
Here, to the reliquary quiet of the Rockies

They are all come back
They are all come back
With the exquisite soul of Lucia
They are all come back
Here … to the quiescent calm of the Rockies

She's brought the blossoms of Cinco de Mayo
the wishbones of her Andean doves
the metaphysical poppies of Machu Picchu
Here, to the quietus of the Rockies

Lucia, her essential earth, Lucia's come back
Her words with the fragrance of lilacs
Her words with the full moon's resonance
Her words with the full sun's resilience
Return here, to the monumental quiet of the Rockies

Ah the blossoms of Cinco de Mayo
the wishbones of her Andean doves

the metaphysical poppies of Machu Picchu
the great stone testament of the Rockies

The world, the whole sad world
The battered jockeys of California
The drunken dentists of Texas
The eternal laundromats of Albuquerque
All here, here at the memorial psalter of the Rockies

Peter Michelson

Midwinter Observance

   for K & H

This is the day of the Saint,
And yet before the Saint
Girls lit great fires—

They leapt unburnt
Into their lovers' arms,
Redeeming with such leaps

Our souls from greater fires.
The green world too
Thereby would thrive

And grains grow richly golden …
*Come pears and cherries
And all sweet fruits …*

*A blessing on these fecund boughs,
A flowering in their sacred roots …
Come pears and cherries*

And all sweet fruits …
So sang the ancient folk
And feasted by their fires

Ah yes their gifted lovers gave
The very gift they got
And all the world was quickened.

And still when lovers
Leap the fires they kindle
We gather in the circle

Of their blest light and heat,
And in that bright incontinence
Our ancient amnesty's complete.

Peter Michelson

A Recollection, Miraculous Jack's Melodious Knack

Slick as randy goats does Jack's art
scamper up escarpments and leap
sierras from peak to pointy peak.
It can shinny rivulets and spiney falls alike
to valley floors and lie or lay awaiting
herons great and blue or egret white,
articulate a finch's golden feathers,
espy a warbler's flaming hue, the while
high and higher at the wonder of
how nature's numbers rhyme eschew and screw.

Jack can cackle kachoo cajole or knock
the 8-ball in a guarded corner pocket and
with cool esprit evoke algebraic ontology
to ecliptic implications.... Here at the edge
of these flatiron rocks I've seen Jack
translate cormorant to commonweal exulting how
naturally koans and so-ons go yodeling on
and on in German, grousing, yes, and make it stick.
There, the white-tailed ptarmigan, he said, or so I thought.
It might have been a white-veiled paradigm.
As when he was nowhere near Oraibi nor
the sandy shores of Ilium
arguing with something Plato said.

May be that logos is the shadow of what happens,
But let that pass. I say nay sing that Jack's
melodious attack on all the downhead retro
acts counteracting natural humors
has served civility with joyful artifacts
combating all the pestilence, wars and avarice

and ecocide persistent through postmodern years.
Where presidents and such pretenders present
Cupidity and fear cultivating atavistic strife,
Jack's melodious knack cuts the carp like Alexander's knife.

Peter Michelson

A%%FTER THE F%%ALL

>
for L. H.

Of quadrupeds there is this kind called horse
you sit atop distinctly at your peril.
Beware, though riders admire its gaited force

its species is *caballus,* genus *Equus,*
and it evolved by staying mainly feral.
Among four-leggeds is this kind called horse

the very name of which evokes the source
for what we saddle up or harness, i.e., power.
Beware, though riders admire its gaited force

the horse's origin is prehistoric.
It feels wildness to its very marrow
this restless quadruped we know as horse.

The beauty of an appaloosa cayuse
runs counter to a piston's sterile barrel.
Beware, though riders admire its gaited force

it hates combustion's fustian and shies or, worse,
will kick apart contraptions with its heel.
Of quadrupeds there is this kind called horse.
Beware, though writers admire its gaited force.

III

Chronicles of Ceylon

Having seen the Bodhi Tree
in the ancient sacred city,
having seen the poson proceeding
through the ancient royal city,
having attained a great impatience
with the ubiquitous bhikkhus,
having no pretension
to supreme enlightenment,
nor to transcendence
of the four asavas,
and having seen the Lion feed
and the Tiger feed
on the carrion of paradise,
I recite these chronicles
of Ceylon now Sri,
which is to say Resplendent, Lanka
for the pleasure and cognizance
of those disposed to Serendib.
All this more than 20 centuries
after the Sage entered into nibbana
and Krishna sang a Yoga melody.

Peter Michelson

Milady Left Me Pizzicato

That is to say upbeat
with a pluck pluck on the pizzle
to remember her by,
saying, Aybovan.
But don't count your chickens
is what my granddaddy always said,
and there's many a slip
is what the Bard said,
and the blues is blues
until it's not
is what Leadbelly said
who should know and did.
Who also said
if your Lady's any good at all
she's good enough to follow after
even if it's to literally
the Lion's den and Tiger's lair
where the big cats fight
for a woebegone island
sizzling in the old imperial sun,
which is also how I see it
and what I went to do.

Colombo Airport

A foreigner is a tourist,
and a tourist is blood in the water.
Milady meets me, beautiful and astute
as shark repellent.
Still, I make the mistake
of looking like I'm looking
for something I can't find.
This is the third world
where the poor are plentiful
and conspicuously poor.
You are a feature of their horoscope,
that anonymous financial opportunity—
conspicuous and luxuriously white,
Moby Dick surrounded by starving orcas,
a nexus basic as the food chain,
relentless as a cancer.
You are the host.
I remember Elmore's hoarse whisper
at my dry mouthing of the dry bread
that was Emmanuel Tabernacle's wafer,
Don't chew, I gagged
waiting to wash the body
down with the blood.
But you cannot be swallowed whole.
They gather at the river, ravenous.
One grabs the luggage cart I push,
grips as if for life
and gestures mutely.
His pod-mates, rasping in a babble,
whisper hoarsely, *Chew!*
Whichever way I push

Peter Michelson

he won't let go.
His mates' hot breaths are in my face,
700 rupees for a cab.
Elsewhere Milady negotiates a lesser fare.
I steer my mute to her.
His extortion's existential:
I'm mute, you're not,
accounts are balanced out in coin,
how much more or less is up to you.

Rubber Match

His name's Aneil.
He lives down the street.
Every 6 a.m. like a witless coocoo
he rings our front door bell
Rupee is his first demand,
then a litany of all
the English words he knows,
each convertible to cash,
rubber, bottles, paper, trash.
Rubber?
Yuh yuh yuh, his voice is breathy, weird.
We're not sure we hear him right,
though it's not impossible he thinks
he can deal foreign condoms second-hand.
He's a bit peculiar in the head.
His siblings go to school.
He drifts the street all day,
repeats his ritual whenever we appear.
He's maddening but still
as much as we say no,
however great our aggravation,
he persists in his benign demented smile.
As if his demand for rupees rubber or whatever
is after all a salutation.
Whether we say yes or no or go away
we might as well be saying that
indeed the weather's fine.
To derail this looney dialogue
that only Beckett could admire
I buy Aneil a rubber ball.
He gazes at it thoughtfully,

Peter Michelson

then vocalizes something not so much a thanks
as an oddly formal taking of his leave.
He holds the ball up high.
He races down the street.
Next a.m. he rings the bell at six.

We Like Americans

Just as we navigate past a cow
taking a dump on the sidewalk
a corporal in
The Tactical Police Force of Sri Lanka
stops us in our tracks.
Where are we going
What are we doing
Where are we from.
His face is sober.
The English takes some concentration.
An Uzi dangles from his finger
hooked through the trigger guard.
Good evening, he says then. Incongruous.
Good evening, I reply. To the Uzi.

We like Americans, he says,
looking toward his captain thirty feet away.
That's my captain, he says.
Ah good, I say. To the Uzi.
What is our business
Where do we stay.
My one eye's on the Uzi,
the other calculates reply.
He says he wants to pay a call.
Will that be business I inquire.
He doesn't understand, repeats.
A week from Wednesday might be good, I say.
Will that include your friend?
I eye the Uzi,
he his captain in the red beret.
Uh, I say, we'll just be on our way.

Peter Michelson

He nods. His captain, who wears
a sidearm, reaches out.
I freeze midstride.
His gunhand pats my belly,
round as Buddha's own.
If you see Buddha on the road, kill him.
Does that old koan apply?
I hold my breath. The captain grins.
I breathe deep, and we pass by.

First Law of Lankan Dynamics

Recent Lankan arrangements are
that Buddhists slaughter Hindus
who return the favor in kind.
On the other hand, the Hindu cows
continue grazing placidly
in the precincts of
the Buddha's sacred shrines.
And, as is their habit,
they are often indiscriminate
with the contents of their bowels.
But the Buddha's legendary poise
stays poised,
and his wrathful sidekicks count to ten.
The holy cows crop the weeds and fertilize
while the old Tathagata smiles.
It all works out.
You'd think someone might have noticed.

Peter Michelson

Setting Up Shop

He's at the one crosswalk
from the Galle Face Green
and its old colonial hotel,
the only way you can get anywhere.
Somewhere between 39 and 90,
he deliberately unstraps his leg,
makes an oddly graceful sweep
for balance with his stumpy thigh
and squats with incisive skill.
He sets the leg before him
standing upright in its shoe.
The leather harness makes its own demand.
Tonight he's staked out the space
before that rachitic nursing mother
with the monkey child,
who's setting up across the street.
You could pass by but don't
before he's opened shop.
He looks straight ahead
not at you or anyone.
He chants in sing-song Sinhalese,
lifts up his gnarly palm.
The cadenced rattle of its seed coins
announces business has begun.

Nature or Nurture

The rumor is that if it's not
done to them at birth
the premier beggars mutilate themselves.
For the certified blind who
hire kids to hustle alms,
or the man with no arms
who speaks English and is in your face
all over town, or the one with two stumps
lashed to a cart, or the woman
with ulcerating wounds and two pathetic urchins,
or the many others with similar stigmata
this is plausible.
But the guy with no fingers
except a horny digit
twisting from his palm
like a mole's snout?
Now *that* design goes way beyond
even the most inventive
of career calculations.

Peter Michelson

Pitching the Catch and Vice Versa

This CEO is smoother than a custard
cooler than the treacle in his mouth
could not agree he more with human rights
not he of course including laborers
indeed a union proper as for grievances
this company stands ready firm discussion and
redress yes could not more agree human
rights imperative as treacle on his tongue
but then the other hand this strike these pickets
at the gate he quite agrees of course
but then the company its obligations
in fact a hinderance the government
the war the national defense agrees
he quite contractual imperatives
quite this strike contrary to the law
the government the national defense
contractual emergency regulations
police imperative prefer of course
discussion and redress unfortunate
agrees he quite the boys in jail
unfortunate this picketing the gate
but scabs a bit insulting don't you think
negotiate of course I quite agree
this company ah here's the boy with tea

The Parable of Western Women and the Lankan Lizard

Someone's tagged the lizard Ed.
Rita talks to Ed seductively.
Ed is skeptical....
It's an attitude but
it has served him well.
He stays in the courtyard—
plenty of ants, the cover's good,
and the living is reliable.
But Rita's patient and tempting
and pretty soon he's sitting on her knee.
Meanwhile Frances invites
a pert stray kitten in
to match wits with the household rat.
One thing leads to another
and soon Ed's left Rita's knee
to lounge about the kitchen.
There, while the rat keeps a low profile,
a misfortunate convergence
of Ed with the feline brings
an abrupt end to Ed's romance
to say nothing of his history.
With the right-brain ratiocination
for which they're infamous
the men all say
it just goes to show
that to survive
you have to be a rat.

Peter Michelson

This A.M. in Batti Has Begun

A dog, scrofulous and bony, lies
inert beside Lloyd's Road.
The raucous crows convene nearby.
Otherwise, the day dawns clear.
Muslim prayers broadcast
the rising sun.
Brightly saried women, men
in dress shirts and sarongs
pad their stately sandaled gait.
Kerchiefed kids in uniform
gaggle on toward school.
They file through the checkpoint on the bridge.
Neighborhood goats browse the shoreline trash.
A dainty billy rears and mocks a charge,
remembering some atavistic call.
A bullock cart is overtaken by
a foursome perched upon the family bike.
The parish bell rings the faithful in.
Now the dog has twitched its ear and yawned,
canceling its comment on mortality.
No matter to the shrilly rising crows.
They know whatever route they fly
this hounded landscape's likely to provide
some thing or one with blank and tasty eyes.

Making Book

At the National Museum
rare palmyra-leaf books
are kept in dim glass cases.
In Anuradhapura every other teenage kid
has one or more to sell.
This one's bird-dogged me for half an hour.
Business is slow these days.
But his naive shamelessness
has a certain charm.
He says he's saving up for university
but those in Lanka won't admit him.
They're for the rich he says,
maybe I could get him into M.I.T.
I smile, he grins and shrugs,
as if to say you never know.
He brandishes another palm-leaf book,
4,000 rupees. I raise my brow.
Maybe three would do.
The text is medical he says.
They're always medical I say.
He shrugs and opens to an illustration,
possibly a liver or esophagus.
Are they all the same I say.
He shrugs, he hasn't read them all.
Isn't selling them illegal
or are all these fake I say.
Not fake he says his finger on
the esophagus or liver.
Real palmyra leaf he says real calligraphy.
I mean are they forgeries I say.
He doesn't know the word.

Peter Michelson

When I explain he says Of course.
An authentic forgery I say.
A real copy he retorts and grins.
Just like the Buddha's statuary?
Just like the Buddha's he replies.
Aybovan I say.
He whips out a cloth of stones.
Perhaps I'd like to see some real gems.

Bhikkhu Bashing, Six Bits

These bloody bhikkhus, the cabbie says.
His sentence dangles but reverberates....
In the *Mahavamsa* Buddha is the "Conqueror."
His compassion plays a muted second chair.
That may be why the bhikkhu practice now
balances the sword upon the dharma.
When, as they will, things begin to tilt
the bhikkhus grip the handle
and the Tamils get the point.

The Thera Buddharakkita was
a singular assassin who
took the famous middle way
between killing for the Dharma,
pocketing an ill-earned buck,
and treating his mistress as you might expect.
This doesn't say much for his practice
of the precepts, to say nothing
of monastic disciplines.
But that extraordinary equipoise
does seem to have steadied his aim.

In the faces of the bhikkhus,
the old-line Christian missionaries said,
was a great vacancy.
Father Merton later on admired
the silence of the Buddha's great
stone faces at Polonnaruwa
which knew everything and questioned nothing.
I prefer the poet's appreciation.
But the odd conjunction of these perceptions

Peter Michelson

possibly explains the sanguinary
bhikkhu answer to the "Tamil Question."

When the Venerables say no peace
until the Tamils swarm on Adam's Bridge
back the way they came, that Buddhists
are surrounded to the north and west
by Tamils and on the south by sea,
a Sinhalese agnostic says,
they're fighting battles lost 2,000 years ago.
If the Tamils were invaders
so indeed were Sinhalese.
Ask the Veddhas, though nowadays
they're somewhat hard to find.

Just for the record
a Tamil friend takes me to
a kinder gentler bhikkhu.
Turns out, under his shaved skull
and deceptive suntan,
he was a French New Caledonian.
He didn't carry a parasol.
He didn't pull the Tiger's tail.
He didn't praise Buddhocracy.
And, like old King Asoka,
he thought his fellow Theravadans
were due for some reform.

Now the bhilkus are complaining
that some obscure sect of Christians
is converting poor diseased peasants

with the logic that
they'll live better and longer
if they clean up their act.
The Christian house is not
altogether in order itself,
but when it comes to open sewers
and the marketplace of suchness
the bhikkhus could improve
their competitive edge
by cashing in a few whitewashed dagobas
for some down-and-dirty drainage tiles.

Peter Michelson

MEAN TIMES MEAN DEMEANOR

Cyril is a fisherman,
now an inland refugee from war.
Each night he's hip-deep
in these ancient desert tanks
casting out his net.
Each morning's take will be
20 rupees to the kilo more or less.
He's got four kids in school,
clean uniforms are daily de rigueur
plus the bus fare and a lunch.
By the time the day's begun
at least two kilos of his catch are gone,
if indeed the catch includes as much.
Schooled by Negombo priests
he's proud his English is articulate.
He has an incisive Catholic's view
of Lanka's war between its sects.
Still, he's Sinhala after all.
He knows the local flora—
from margosa for example comes Khomba soap,
which discourages mosquitos.
We talk comparative astronomy, religion,
Lankan economics, education …
the war rides hard on working men,
they don't teach English like they did.…
Three quarters of an hour's walk
and Cyril goes his way as we go ours.
We each agree we'll write.
Today his letter comes.
His writing style's more florid—
"May Almighty God Bless You Very Graciously

Honorable Dear Sir and Madame," it begins.
He recalls our walk, observes
that "Tamil terrorism" goes from bad to worse.
But the bottom line's the top of his agenda,
expenses more than his capacity to earn,
credits and debits itemized.
He hopes we don't misunderstand.
But, in sum, he needs a bicycle,
would we send the cash for one.
That God has blessed our life with peace
is how he ends, and then
the enterprising signature
of a proud and straitened man
whose wager with humiliation
we don't misunderstand.

Peter Michelson

OFFICIAL HABITS

Murder is a universal crime … and habit.
Execution is not a universal crime
but is a widespread habit.
When is official habit criminal?

Corpse and murder link like bread and butter.
The girl or her corpse has disappeared,
a familiar custodial scenario.
Precedent permits proceedings in her absence.

Worse luck still for the defendant,
who's a cop, for if he's innocent
the government is guilty, and
the government is judge and prosecution.

Luckily for it defendant Kandara's
a Mexicano villain look-alike
from Central Casting—sullenly mustached,
a pouty, self indulgent face and shifty eyes.

He's a *prima facie* instance
of a man to whom or from no good
is bound to come, a case from which
justice is unlikely to be wrung.

Still, that's what the victim's peasant family,
sadly lined along a courtroom bench,
so long and rigorously sought.
What do they see, so hopefully, so numb?

Kandara's now a joker in the hand
that his employer didn't want to play
but will, indeed it must. We're here to
watch, the world's eyes, the world's ears.

The World Bank wants justice done.
The World Bank wants clean accounts.
We stand our watch for "human rights."
We take the ironies that come.

In Kandara's unit of the National Police
are fifty guys more or less like him
who are assigned on any given night
to missions more or less like this.

On this given night was Kandara there
or was he somewhere similar
and someone else was there
distinctly similar to him?

Perhaps the point is moot.
For each of many disappearances
more or less like this
there is an unindicted murderer.

The government has played its hand.
Kandara is lying face up on the table.
He has one hope justice doesn't have,
that the victim, as he claims, was JVP

Peter Michelson

and so *de facto* murder was *de jure* execution.
Execution is not a universal crime
but is a widespread habit.
When is official habit criminal?

We all want justice done.
We all want clean accounts.
We stand our watch for "human rights."
We take the ironies that come.

Talking at the Lakeview Inn

By trade a scholar of philosophy
he talks of Tamil culture
and his desperate university amid the war.
The evening breeze chops the wide lagoon,
a moat that keeps the Tigers
from the garden of this modest inn.
He watches, as he speaks, the sun
drop toward the hills beyond the farther shore.
Twilight here is always brief.
By dark he must be gone.
By dark the only motion in the streets
will be the nervous laughter
in bunkered checkpoints
from Sinhalese young men.
His eyes compute the time he has.
The bell of St. Michael's parish tolls.
The mosque broadcasts the evening prayers.
His voice grows more intense,
how Tamil students fear, are ill prepared,
are like his books and manuscripts
the victims of a savage Lankan flux
and contrapuntal soul.
Several crackling rounds of fire
from less than half a mile north
interrupt the flow.
A pause, another burst.
The urgencies compete.
His eyes compute the time.
The light is nearly gone.
He says our time together's precious, too much so
to be distracted by … he waves a hand.

Peter Michelson

It settles on my shoulder, warm.
The intimate affinity of strangers strangely joined.

WAGE-SLAVE WAGES

You can call him *peon* to his face.
They do and there is no offense.
It's all a question of caste
and one I do not ask.
His job is to be our slave
thus proving Marx was right.
I don't want to know
what the pittance is he makes.
He must be touchable
since among his chores
is serving tea and biscuit snacks.
He can't believe I drink this bitter straight.
He'll be no party to
so unnatural an act.
And if to disapprove were in his lexicon
it's what he'd do as well
when I say please or thanks.
He instead exaggerates his bob and shuffle
to facilitate me saving face.
There's no appeal to my colleagues
who think he's acting nature's script
and is too dull to do much else.
My unraveling liberalism
can't take the Oriental pace.
Teach you all I know
and still you don't know nothing
as my old mentor used to say.
And if this peon knows nothing else
he knows a man should know his place.

Peter Michelson

Code of Road Behavior

We clear the checkpoint east of Eravur
and overtake an Army convoy.
The driver's Lankan instinct is to pass,
blind curves notwithstanding.
Slow down, the V-C says, fall back.
The point I say is don't upstage the Army?
The point the V-C smiles is not to get
between the ambusher and ambushee.

Second Law of Lankan Dynamics

The World Bank returns to Lanka.
Peoplization cranks up another notch.
Ditto stock in the Bank of Ceylon
and Lanka Nestles, Lanka Coca-Cola …
Almost everyone can afford
canned milk or Coke.
Choice is first world fruit.
Meanwhile, over in the jungle,
the battered Tamil peasants think
the Tigers might be onto something.
The Tigers think so too,
but they've forgotten what it was.
Knocking off some Muslims
might jog their memory.
They gun them down
on the trains out of Batti
on the busses out of Batti
on the streets of Eravur
they gun them down.
Still they can't remember.
What was it?
They keep firing,
but they can't get it straight.
And they have to keep firing
until they can recall …

Peter Michelson

Enduring Witness, the Mosque at Kattankudi

Muhammad wheels us through
these incisive narrow lanes,
the same the Tigers took
grim, methodical and quick
to yet another keening mosque—
a plaque inscribes each name and age,
one hundred three in all, the youngest six.

An ancient man, survived, displays his wound
and shrugs—Allah's will, Muhammad says,
a pillar saved the old imam and him.
The walls, the floor, the splintered struts
all bear witness to the old man's memory ...
Prostate, pious forehead to the floor,
what could he see or know
who only recollects a sudden fusillade,
a hundred strangled prayers in stricken throats,
and then as now a silence
punctuating groans of brute mortality.

Outside, a gaggle of small boys—
One quickly darts to touch my arm
like counting coup.
His buddies giggle. Muhammad smiles.

At Muhammad's home a photo record
of the massacres in grisly Kodachrome.
I set aside these documents.
My witness cannot bear so much.

Now, though curfew's drawing on,

custom's mercy mandates tea.
Muhammad's wife quietly attends
with sugared cashews, treacle cakes, watalappan
then, backing off, stands smiling by.
The children, curious, are let in.
First of course the son, age six,
then the slightly older girl, shy
but strangely bolder than the boy.
Then cousins, uncles, aunts,
until at last another ancient man …

I turn away and see the photos
open on the couch and turn away again.
Back at the mosque, marked by low stone walls,
the dead are filed in pebbled graves.
Meanwhile we are, too like the Tigers, quick—
our fragile witness borne
upon those durable imperatives
grace and hospitality.

SELECTED POEMS
PLAINSONG

from *The Eater* (1972)

Advertisement

       Reader, my guess is ...
you needs a whetting to your tastes
           not to mention a wondering
        to your pander. You're

   standing by the pomeshelf
in one—no more than two—of the twenty bookstores that
      sells poems across this great

   land (Reader, I want it understood here and now that
rumours about my competitors notwithstanding—those
   nameless and incompetent
        assholes—I
   like, nay *love,* my country: I
have never gone back where I came from, much
        to my poor, overburdened mother's
   relief; I, even tho the
army scorned me, never
burned my draft card; and
      twice when I was in trouble I
   called the cops rather than a hippy—though
I did once ask one for a match, *which*
he did not have, showing
what you can expect from them!) and

      you wonders should you buy a book by
Gary Snyder or Don Lee or Lawrence Ferlinghetti! Don't
       do it, Reader. They are freaks.

   To a man they love *other things*
more than their country! More

Peter Michelson

                    than their mother! And
don't buy that book of Immortal Poems of the English
                        Language. It
is filled with Beauty, Reader. The opiate of the rich.

                Buy this very book you
            are holding in your hands. Patronize
                    us Reader, we
          are a small and dwindling group who

                  love our mothers, who
                  love our country, who
         despise drugs, who don't, like decadent
Salomes, want things handed to us on a platter.

          Don't drive us to freakerie, Reader.
                Buy this book.

        The pains, Reader, the pains we have taken
      to make a pure American product. This
             book was printed in Indiana,
              Indiana, Reader, the

          heart of the country.
          In a union shop.
          For a union wage.
    Printed, for your protection,
        by American printers, who will not
                print lies, slander or filth. Not

               in Europe or Japan, like
        some of your publishers, where
                   taste and labor is cheap and
     the dollar is drained. Moreover,

                     the price is right, Reader,
             a fair price for
               good American-made merchandise. A
reasonable margin of profit for the publisher, Reader,
  you can understand that,
     he's a business man,
       it's the American way.

       And Reader I promise,
   cross my heart and hope to die,
that whatever money I make I will spend right here

            in the good old U.S. of A. For
mortgages, cars, color televisions, credit cards, and interest.

    Not, like a lot of your poets,
        fritter it away
galavanting around the world
            badmouthing the fatherland.

    There are no foreign words here, Reader,
not one! I
        don't even *know* any foreign words.

    Try it, Reader, you'll *like* it.

Peter Michelson

                The writing in this book is
    "bawdy, wildly funny, and sometimes serious and direct."
                  That's a *quote,* Reader,
                not some huckster or
          fancy intellectual snob critic, but

              a quote in a country newspaper
      in plain American
by an ordinary salt-of-the-earth citizen like yourself.

            Wildly funny, Reader,
                sometimes serious and direct.
  Oh Reader
          I hear America singing.
            True, a little bawdry
         but we Americans know about that
don't we Reader,
a little spice but
        basically good clean fun.

              Man to man stuff, Reader,
          not for your sissy queers
        and romantics, man
to man, for red-blooded Americans,
                  in the locker room,
              behind the barn.

    Reader, we're Americans together.
I know you. You know me.
      We understand each other.
You'll eat the eyes out of this book!

        Consume it
with a friend, Reader, with your wife, your husband—eat
        chew eat chew eat chew, he
reads that, you read Oh
            how I'd like to, it
        makes me feel soooo good to
    and you me tooo

            be sure you read it
            out loud, together
        at home around the fire, a
            family book

        eatcheweatcheweatchew(Oh
how I'd like to)eatcheweatcheweatchew(it
makes me feel so good to)eatcheweatcheweacthew (and
        you me tooo)eatcheweatcheweatchew. . . . .

        Get it, Reader?
            Wild fun?!
        Don't you feel *good?*
            When you ask,
    what does it all mean,
            must the poet always answer
                less and less?!

    No, No, Reader, a thousand times NO.

    It's high time we accentuate the positive, the
good things in this great land of ours—Oh

Peter Michelson

        Reader, Reader,
          what more can I say . . . . What More . . . .

   Please, Please, Reader
   BUY AMERICAN!

       Notary Sojac, Reader, from
          The Eater

The Eater

Euclid alone has looked on Beauty bare.
    —Edna St. Vincent Millay

Euclid be damned
God damn his eunuch forms
I require shape for consummation, bare:
fruits have it
apples
in their erotic skins
but plums too and pears
and even dates
incite my flair
for appetite

The business of the eater
    is to eat,
be opulent in ruminating
    flesh and pulp:
Let his organs operate
    at will—
a split sphincter is
an affirmation still:

Let tooth and tongue go
    bare, dredging juice and rind—
Yesss   this world's succulent:
    Tooth! Tongue!
Forth upon the firmament!
    Eating to and fro in it,
melons roundly ripe and fair,
    hot meat wet and rare—

Peter Michelson

Lip lascivious, soft you Tongue, reverently
    and Tooth you most lustfully must ravage!

      Fair's fair, plump's plump,
      but fat's the better thing—
      It is the eater's gorge(ousness)
      his gluttony, I sing

The eater prospers so
to eat and eats to
prosper fatly
Let him who will
go sveltly cloaked and trim,

the eater must pursue
    his plan;
assault the symmetries of shape—
      the shapely grapes
      incline to sin,
      and a withered one,
      however chaste,
      is after all
      a flaccid skin
so the eater must
    pursue his plan
assaulting shape
    as best he can

The business of the eater is
    to consummate

The business of the eater is
    to generate

The eater has prodigious plans
Ahh, yes, the eater is a lovely man.

Peter Michelson

Going Hungry at Our Lady's Place

                      At Notre Dame
             today is
       the Feast of the Absorption—
All work stops—

                Though brazen Moses'
        angry toes grip and
              finger prick the
                      muddled sky,
     Though infidel riveters—or
          believers
        moonlighting—
    hammer home our
 lady's newest sporting
house,
     Though prophecy and
       sporting life
            make hay, the

      library—its
  gold and quartzite Christ
upstaging Cecil B.
     DeMille—is
        dark beneath that
          slab-faced
        blessing.

              I want books

                    and curse the dark
               beneath Christ's brow—my
                    calendar toasts
                         only
                      famine—What
                         now?

        Before me, Moses
glowering Christ's love, behind,
            the riveting's unholy
       clatter—with
                business so abruptly

                    altered
                my day's coherence is
         displaced—idled and irreverent, I
                              am much
                       ungraced.

Peter Michelson

It's cold, a ragged Chicago wind off the lake, and—after drinks at Ricardo's where we went to see the mad Ivan Albright painting behind the circle bar because an artist friend told me to—Susan's coat is too slight. So, for no reason, not knowing her well enough even to know if she would smoke it, I light a cigar for her, and go off to get the car, leaving her with the black doorman and Mexican hatcheck lady and the cigar. When I get back, the doorman has asked her why she is smoking the cigar. Why not, she says. He laughs. So does the hatcheck lady. So does Susan. Her smoking the cigar makes them all, in that moment, happy. They will never be unhappy in that moment. The doorman is so pleased he forgets to do his job. Susan opens the door for herself, still laughing and puffing the cigar. She brings some of the happiness into the car.

The Eater Goes 1) West, or 2) to the Movies

    Here sand throbs and
              cactus pricks
        the flaccid air. In
          such glare beside
    this burning stone   a
diamondback rasps and
      coils just where
         I'd walk.   In

  the movies   Randolph
        Scott rides up   hard
lipped and drills long muscley
    (broad grins grinned
  here) drills ol' snake,
        reins up
        hard,
       swinging long

    levied   (Mr. Scott's
     wardrobe by Levi Straus, the
man who won/dressed the west) I say he
               swings long levied leg over
    puckered buckskin haunch pivoting
in stirrup and
    holsters steely   *long* (grin)
ol' Colt .45 before
      he hits the ground im-
        pressive in dust
      cloud
  touching thumb and trigger

      finger, to brim and
              smiles *howdy ma'am,* stretch-
ing lips across his
        froooty white teeth, tight
            sphincter emitting no
sign of exertion from
    man or beast (fan-
              tastic so cooool), while
I (ooh sin, shame, and degra-
        dation) I
           present my parts (blush). Her
    parts are blushing says lab
        technician making no-
        tation and adjusting elect-
        rodes. Her parts, he
        muses, blushing hmmmmmmm
    But

Here / Now / Among
      these waiting sands   I
      suck in and
loathe this air
    face this
        snake a-
lone, much too afraid to
        fight too paralyzed for
            flight—hang
    dog to know that should
  I ride I'd be
  obliged to sit
astride—so . . . . say:

is him a hairy- or a slick-palmed her-
    maphroditic Grace reclined awhile
            beguiled at
                that cocked snake and
        me ungunned, face
            to mortal face?

Peter Michelson

Whatever Happened to Rita Hayworth

    was that she said to Jack Lemmon   then
                                                  a punk kid

       trapped
   by a fallen steel girder
             in the basement of   the *U.S.S. Heart*

             of Darkness, where
       he keeps stroking his beard and saying,
"This too has been one of the dark places of the earth,"

    until Joseph P. Levine Presents,
 the producer, goes apeshit   shrieking
      "Punk,
shave that fucking beard,"   and kicks
      a steel girder which, this being
            Hollywood, collapses on the kid

     which is how
       he got stuck there
 in the aftermath of a sinking ship in the first place,
      when Rita

           Hayworth sashays (that
     is to say she threw all her pounds from
 the hips on down, alternating
                  hips, because
it ain't watcha got it's whatcha do with whatcha got, which is the

  story of how
Rita Hayworth survived—or did

             she?—into the age of Brigitte

                              Bardot), howsoever
that may be she sashays up (zoom front, crotch/pan back, ass) to
                          the kid, pinned
                    and wriggling, up to his
          anal aperture in rising bilge but still
                          Marlovian:

"And this too has been one of the dark places of the earth,"

              he says, not
                       unmindful that Zukini or
         Buggeratti or Fellatio or some other arty Wop
might wander into the Roman Cinema after a sportive night
              with
     decadent aristocrats ("plays Bach like that,
                    and shot hisself!"   "Couldn't make
             C sharp on his organ."   "Pretty fucking tragic,

                  that's what!") and ogling
       huge inscrutable one-eyed flounders like they do

              and discover
           the Lemmon to star in a far-out   Itralian
                                       version of *When Moses
Saw God's Hinder Parts, or The Sweet Smell of Success,* but

           Miss Hayworth does
                her job the best she can,   and

Peter Michelson

                                              takes to licking his
                                  palm (suggestively!) between the

        index and foreplay fingers across his life line to
the wrist where she lays a couple
                lascivious swirls on his pulse,   saying

"Are you sure you can't get free tonight?"

                                          whereupon
                            the kid, aspiring al-
               ways to high art, thinks he is in Martial's
mac Lure play and
      says, "Fanfuckintastic! I
            think I can erect
                an excuse." Which he does, saying,
        "I thought I could," and, easily disengaging

            himself from the
     girder, he figures from there
       on it's all downhill,   only
                    to hear Rita say, as

he approaches her with
palpitating eyes,   *"You don't want me!"* (which,
              strictly speaking, was not true but
          was all right to say for the purposes of
                the picture which after all, rather than
       Miss Hayworth, is what the kid was supposed
            to be making,
        showing that Hollywood knows about

art, contrary to appearances, when
it can have Rita Hayworth tell such a
beautiful though obvious lie, not
to mention not mixing business with
pleasure which the ugly rumor
about it is)
"You don't want me! (she says) / *Armies* have marched over me!"

Now *this*, strictly speaking, *was* true,
though it is not clear
from the celluloid
nature of the statement whether she

meant those of Genghis
Khan's cousin

Alley Oop Khan, whose armies
then as now were the scourge of the far west and
who was so named because even though
he was from Caldwell, Idaho

he could
jump very high and
thus himself became the Black Scourge

of the Czar's key stadium at
catching passes—many of which were disgracefully

thrown
at Miss Hayworth (a better than average
receiver), though some, this being the home of

Peter Michelson

                            the Mattachine Society, were
               also thrown at Hustling Hugh McElhenny (a less
than average receiver), misnamed by a hopeful gay publicity

                                    agent for the 69ers but
                       since traded for Peter Orlovsky, Allen
          Ginsberg, and two
future neophyte monks (all considered

           good receivers) to Gary
      Snyder's Kyoto Bearcats, where, known as
The Voice of the Pink Peril, Hustling Hugh announces

                      the Bearcats slashing
meditational style of play in the zen manner, for
                     instance—"October afternoon, a
                 certain slant / off
              tackle, line/
            past, Ah
           light."

Or whether she meant
       the armies of Frankie Sinatra which
            then as now occupied Chicago and Lake Tahoe, because
                 Miss Hayworth
occasionally had delusions
of grandeur and thought she was Ava Gardner,   under which
                    misinformation she
      once married a Mexican matador, only to be
   deserted
when he moved up to Barcelona

             in the Three-I
       League, at which point she   thought she was

                    Marilyn Monroe and
   married an outfielder, who it turned out was good hit no
           field (or, as crazy
       Leonard used to chant—"Who
                can run and hit and throw / Better
                    than his brother Joe? / Why,
                        it's Dominic DiMaggio!), so

           still looking for
   a real passer, and by this time   supposing she was
                           Jane Russell, she married
               a quarter back, a tough cookie but much given to
       passing water   which was not
                one of her things, so for no
   clear reason whatsoever she decided she was Leontyne Price

           and married (much
       to everyone's distress) an Italian tenor,   alas
                           a vestigial castrato,
   and, since one Italian tenor is very like another, things
       seemed to be

               going in circles, so
       her agent put her out to stud, announcing
                           that
                       the whole thing had got
           out of control. But,

Peter Michelson

    inasmuch as she
  moved around to a lot of studios scholars have to this day

      been ignorant of
    which army she meant—Frankie's or
  Aly's (as Miss Hayworth affectionately called him
in happier days), or whether she might not have meant, inscrut-

    ably, Audrey Hepburn's
in *War and Peace* or Pamela Mason's army of women's liberation
       in *The Desert Fox* or

    perhaps even
  Bogart's dried-up little one in *Sahara*. There

        is much dispute. Lately
the whole thing has been turned over to J. Edgar Hoover, who

     with full federal support
    has been taking plaster foot casts from the

  parade grounds
of *all* armies on earth, real and imagined, and
    comparing them with the individual footprints of
      all the *people*
    on earth, real and imagined, to
be used as evidence when the time comes. These

   plaster footprints,
along with the pornography he confiscated from

                    Copenhagen (as
        being a threat to the defense perimeter of America)

    and a complete recording
                of all telephone conversations in the world

    for the past twenty-five
years, he is storing in King Farouk's tomb, which
        by order of Spiro Agnew   the Israelis

                appropriated from Egypt
as not only a center of filth, decadence, and unchristian

        behavior, but
also as an undeniable gathering place of Egyptian nationals

                which not even
        the Russians denied. And that
by and large is whatever happened to Rita Hayworth.

Peter Michelson

Getting Hustled in a Laramie Bar

Fantastic!
          Laramie! Gay?
Blows (so to speak) my mind,   in

    the face of all
this sullen, uptight cowboy
        virility.   Must

          be from
     Chicago, New York, L.A.
No,   says he's from Big Piney, Wyoming.

   A curly-headed, burly-
      buttocked student at
     the university of Wyoming, home
of the Cowboys.   Plump enough to play football.

  Why me?
(Discreet Art Models, Inc.
  present Pete—fat, bald, white, 33, straight,
indifferently hung, no interest in leather or discipline—
     now traveling in the west;

    Come on guys, get
  this one while he's in your town!)   Fucking
     faggot's got no taste.   Steps

 up to the bar
    just like a real
person, catches my eye:

                    "Hi," he says,
        "you at the university?"   Then some bullshit
                from me about teaching, etc.
                which he is obviously
                            not

interested in.   Then
        more bullshit from me   about   what does he do
                            (student, secondary edu-
                            cation, graduating, going—where
                else?—to San Francisco) which he is also

                    not interested in.
        "You (i.e., me) live around here?"   "Live by
            yourself?" (moves over two barstools
                    next to me and starts vaguely
                        subtle game of kneesies)

        "Get lonely, living
alone?"   Shit, there must be some *Explorer*
        Scout Handbook for queers that
                    gives a standard
                            routine.

                        But the kid
        can't   quite   figure me out: AC or DC?

                    Finally,
            "You straight?" I confess.
        "Sorry about that." I give him my best
                    well-what-the-fuck-forget-it shrug.

           "Let's keep it between
us."   Cosmopolitan assurance   from me.   He

                              waits a decent interval,
            about 7 seconds, and, as I'm
       about to say something insane   like how
does a cute little dyke like you   make it   in a town like this,

            he splits, off to
       shake his burly buttocks in a
                 frug or twist or something with a college
            chick. Does she, japing her
                 ass around the

       floor, know he prefers me
                       to it?   How about that cowboy, does he?

            No.   It's between us. Him,
       jabbing his well-zipped dick at the chick (maybe, being

                       a native mountain man, he makes it
            with everything—bears and coyotes, too), and

me, watching my only chance
       in Laramie for (literally) a piece of ass   jerk on
                              with his second choice.

       Oh well, things are looking up.
       Shit, a place that breeds indigenous queers can't be all bad.

Hungry Eye at the Flin Flon (Union Pier, Michigan)

Drummer, band, raucous roadhouse
rhythms—girls coiffured, manicured, petite
teenage chic, jeans.   Boys
indisputably Aryan,
clean. Hausfraus—bland and
sagging—hoard their beer, wait glumly
for foxtrots, each other.
Schlitz flicks asteroids through
the dark, Hamm's glows eternal
Gitchee Gumee, and at the bar
the baptized hunch and over-
hang their stools.   GENTS and LADIES
glowing brutal orange diffuse
democratic auras of latrine ...

From this you
rise and dance Diana,
Aphrodite—your

torso contours Bacchic
graces, such bones / such flesh transform

these mortal places, you
dance, smile and Cleopatra's walk

you mimic, laughing, mock
this myth, my need: your
magnitude of leg, of
hip, hair, and shoulder prove

Peter Michelson

            a goddess once was real, you
        bring a bronze to life, a
                    vision richer, older—your
            sweeping poniard
               fingers rake my
strings—ragged down below, above my demon sings

                  erotic
            at the swirl your hair
       in gloried orange and bluelit brings.... Your

   sandaled instep arcs   and
        flexing
     rams my eye a rivet hotly

          up your seam ...
       eyes like molten dreams
along your Levi seams find your

            shadowed secret tautly
                  molded spots: that
    moving marbles me, but
motion moves a motion if even only air—your

             eyes ignite
      a motion all men long to wear ...   my

               apparition are you
        in this precarious night?   Or

are you incarnate here?
in this unlikely place,   in
                this uncertain light

Peter Michelson

I Dream Profuse

Panther Pam, extravagant in public,
strips—fifteen pair of eyes, intense
with nonchalance, anticipate each new
exhibit of her charms and strain uneasy,
waiting for her black and velvet groin
in two/four time to rape their fantasies.
Pam facilitates imagination …
the lights turn green and blue and grimly white,
the darkening drummer drums the driving time,
Pam's rhythmic fingers smooth her mocha skin—
her glowing chocolate torso draws me in …

I feel with her, I dance I dance I must,
she flaunts with me, her haunch she swivels lust
and strokes, her nipple rising to her touch—
those practiced hands obscenely promise much.

Perspiring now I know that she is more
than such a lust as mine prepares me for—
but heat and lights infuse my sweating glands
and I too dance obscene as she demands.

Flannel, my mouth my tongue too thick to cry
I ache, sweat, Sweet, I ache—deny
her sweet, my ache to suck her body dry

Contempt she laughs my fumbling heart
in blatant loving private shows her arts
and laughing smacks her lips her lewdly parts

In heave my hips by her directing hands
and dance I too as she obscene demands …

In dance I joy my Pam to make I scheme
and follow beat at cymbal clang I dream
profuse and caper carnal caper thrust
I steamy pour my magnifying lust
in sweat I joy says rattlesnare and drum
she visions me and fear I sometime come
to face her facing out and sheeny skin
she laughs me sweating breathing hard is sin—
I frighting does she seek my secret smell
wherewith my fetished brain in damn to dwell
me will she give me loving pleasure such
her hands her lips as promise seek me much
I want I fear in rage her massive beauty
jangle sings me husband father duty
halts her hungry breath alluring hands
I dance dance dance as drum and she demand
the snare and clang go *stop*.

                    I gape as caught
my panther dancing there is dancing not
she Chesire-mocks my dreaming wet and hot.

Peter Michelson

The Eater, Impotent

she smiled

among the others and
interrupting, neither graceless
nor gracefully, she

spoke it does not matter what
praises of my poems. And,

as she amused me,
I laughed,
observing how thoroughly she was there.

Then, speaking of what
matters now or does not
matter now, she

gave a gift,
inscribed deliberately—

Was it then
perhaps the gift, and
my receiving,
deliberately,

asking her name, her address
with what purpose I do not now
nor did I know, for

she was neither beautiful
nor stunning

        in any way but that
    she was there in such reality,
                and young.

And when as of course I did I called,
she said,

        you may bring some wine, not
    too pretentious nor yet
                too mean, a wine, how

        shall I say, just suitable
    for the occasion.   And,

as I apparently amused her
and she quite clearly me,
we laughed.

    Perhaps the laughter, then,
and the gift—giving.

        Some thing we sought
    to share. Yes,
yes some simple thing we hoped

        that hovered graciously
                to guide us through the
    anarchies we
breathe inexorably as air.

Peter Michelson

        She received me
     more formally,
a silken scarf brightly in her hair,
       an avocado shawl—

       as if to say,
"respecting forms, their due,
we may address disorders, we
            may risk the sultry air."

      She
  brought glasses then
and cheeses on a board.

From grasses of my choosing she devised exotic cigarettes.

    So we drank and smoked and
talked of this and that.   She

                read poems to me
        through the pungent air.   I spoke
it does not matter what
      praises of her poems—

                  something perhaps
             of fire, something
              perhaps
                    of care. And

      though I
  do not speak of love,   there

was between us / what was penetrable / a thing we shared.

               And on this bridge
  I moved to her   languidly
                            through the conscious air.

  And
as I moved to her   she moved   it
                      is true almost
            imperceptibly, yet *she moved to me.*

Each of us, then, moved.
Deliberately. And
    there followed such
  doings as you may guess between
      our lips and teeth
        and tongues,
      the

        moving of her body beneath my hands.
        And
    there was between us still
the gift—

I bore her gifts
    as you have guessed.
  And it is true / I lusted after giving.

        But,
  as my lips caressed her throat, she
locked my head in her strong arms (for she

Peter Michelson

was tall and strong) and
crooned a fearful croon ...

    who are you
 and who am I, and what do we desire—who are you
        and who am I, and what do
you, do I desire—and

       Yes, remove my clothes, she said,
  beneath this candle's veiled light
     that you may never leave
       for having known this
     auspicious night.

   And yet she held me fast
     and feared the fire,
crooning low and terribly
   of desire ...

  Do not she said Abandon me Abandon
    me Abandon me do not she said
   Abandon me Abandon me Abandon me, Ah
     yes, you must.
      Abandon me ...

  And holding tight,
    tight she crushed / from me air
     and sight, she made
a trance—gripping, gripping me / as if we danced our
         lives' last dance:

                    and yet I felt
                myself abandoned there   as
        if naked straddling naked air,   I
                    sought beneath her shawl and

dress I sought with
            stroking of her skin   I
        with such manipulations reached
    to touch and touching know what spectres wracked the

                soul within her
            supple skin.   For
        I had gifts I longed to give therein.

                But,
            though I held her body in my arms, and
though my touching made her moan,   I

                    knew she was no longer there. I
                felt my psyche too
    like hers at large and moving freely from my will; it

                followed her
            in choreographies
        I could not comprehend.   And

            though she moaned
    and writhed beneath my plunging hips

Peter Michelson

                it was as if
          we wrestled in some baffled
                        sexless brawl, where,

                in my trance of wine and smoke and
     lust, my senses spiraled
    and my thick fingers
  mauled the promise
      of the night.... still

        I sought
    that hot wet fabled place
      of fabled
        grace, and
our lunging bodies grappled

            jaggedly and arched, our
    only union
           stress, our
bodies straining as the broken
  eagle strains against the

failure of its flight,

  and my distending need
buckled beneath the chaos
    of my blood,

    draining from my limbs and heart and
      balls until

        the turbine of my brain screamed
so shrill that all
            my body's timbers trembling announced

          the slacking
      of my prick and spine and skull—

my lust collapsed, my
          clot of body congealing
on the floor.

                What
          gifts now? What
              has a man to give,   a
                          mush of consciousness

                alone,
            afloat precariously
and groping limply for some storied shore.

     Weak and drenched
I left her thus, yes, abandoned
                    abandoned
       to her crucible of dreams,
    I left her thus, abandoned to her

       fitful sleep, I
left her thus, as she had me,
           abandoned,
      undelivered of my gifts, remembering

Peter Michelson

                the touch
        of mine upon her tongue, I left
remembering, for still I drift and grope among the
                      rumored graces of the young.

Remembering May 4, 1970

dead as door mice, dead as door mats
dead in spite of...

their silliness and smiles...
            —John Matthias

Susan Saxe shot a policeman. Perhaps she didn't shoot him. The newspaper said she did. Perhaps, if she shot him, she shot him because he was a pig. Maybe she thought, "policemen are pigs." So she shot him because it's all right to shoot a pig. Perhaps she shot him because she wanted a revolution. Perhaps she didn't shoot him or want a revolution. The newspaper said she did. Perhaps she didn't shoot him because she thought he was a person acting like a pig and she was confused, so she didn't shoot him. Perhaps he was a person acting like a pig. Maybe she thought the world would be a better place if she shot him. Maybe she just wanted to rob the bank (the newspaper said she shot him while she robbed a bank) and he didn't want her to rob the bank, so she shot him. Maybe he thought the world would be a better place if she didn't rob the bank.

She wrote this poem (the newspaper printed a poem and said she wrote it) and said silly things like that she didn't love her mother and that "I must have intensity." Perhaps she shot him because she was silly. Or perhaps she shot him because he was silly. Maybe she thought it was silly to be a policeman, so she shot him. Maybe he thought she was a girl and shooting him didn't seem like a thing a girl would do and she thought that was silly so she shot him. Also she said (the newspaper said) "I have no illusions that I will survive the revolution." Perhaps she thought he would shoot her and when he didn't she didn't know what to do so she shot him. He didn't survive the revolution. The revolution is for the people but lots of people won't survive it. Maybe the revolution is for somebody else. It is not for greedy people.

Peter Michelson

Maybe she thought he was greedy. Maybe she thought he was greedy and mean and shooting him was all right. Maybe he thought she was greedy and mean (the newspaper said she was robbing the bank) but wasn't sure whether it was all right to shoot her so she shot him instead.

John has a new baby daughter, Laura. She is greedy and mean. Her mother's nipples are very sore and her mother is very tired because Laura won't sleep at night and cries instead. Laura doesn't care about her mother's nipples or how tired she is. John's other daughter is two. She is also mean and greedy. Also she is silly. I have two daughters. They are greedy and mean and silly. So am I. So is John. Greedy … Mean … Silly …

from *When the Revolution Really* (1984)

I
Notes from the PRC

When the Revolution Really, Reconsidered

The Chinese say the revolution
is still in progress.
Public transport indicates
there's still a ways to go.
Chinese buses are Hobbesean
time capsules moving implacably
through the Four Modernizations
and Several Courtesies Campaigns.
Late-boarding octogenarian grandmothers
in terminal stages of pleurisy
are obliged to stand until they crumple.
As for waiting patiently while they get off,
between the masses waiting to disembark
and the masses waiting to board,
when the doors open
it's a 20-megaton contradiction among the people.

Peter Michelson

WHO EVER DOESN'T LOVE THE PEOPLE

The customary sentiment here,
articulated by white Western liberals,
is that the Chinese *people* are terrific, *but* ...
The fact is
that the *ratio* of terrific Chinese
is about the same as you'd expect
in Gringos, Frogs or Dagos.
The variant *impression* seems due
to the sheer quantity of Chinese,
i.e., a typical confusion of quality with volume.
Though, given that predisposition,
it's not impertinent to note
that about three quarters of
the world census is
of other shades and, increasingly, persuasions.
As for the customary *adversative conjunction,*
it's a little like Harry Truman saying
the *people* of Hiroshima are terrific, *but* ...

How Spring Comes to China

For the Chinese, Spring is an act of will. First they have Spring Festival, which begins at the end of January. They don't wait around for the warm weather, they go right after it at the coldest time of year. They buy some new clothes, clean house, go visit the relatives and eat a lot of dumplings. The racier ones hit up on Mao Tai, a wine formerly used to embalm emperors. Those who remain vertical have parades and dragon dances. The dragon is to let Winter know that it's time to think about shoving off, the Chinese have had enough.

This goes on for about a month, while it's colder than the proverbial witch's mammary. The last night of Spring Festival all of China becomes a free fire zone for firecrackers and spectacles of aerial bombardment. This is in case the dragon didn't make its point. At 11 p.m. everybody goes to bed.

At 6 a.m. the next morning they all hit the streets, a billion people with brooms, shovels, pruning shears and all that kind of paraphernalia. It's still colder than you know what, but the Chinese are not deceived. This is just another contradiction to be solved. They shovel the snow away from the trees and shrubs and take off the straw mat winter wraps. It doesn't matter if it's a blizzard, that' s what they do. A billion people have taken off three layers of long underwear and rolled up their sleeves.

They shovel and sweep and prune and plant. By noon Winter gives up. Everywhere else it's still February, but in China it's Spring, because Spring is when you take off your long underwear and roll up your sleeves. Winter makes a couple of snarls like an old yaller dog, but he knows he's whipped. A billion Chinese have taken off their long underwear and that's that. It's been going on for hundreds of years, maybe thousands. Who knows when Peking Man decided to take off his long underwear. Small wonder the Chinese became communists. For the Chinese, Spring is an act of will.

Peter Michelson

A Possibly Salutary Application of Chinese Jurisprudence

According to the principle
In the Beginning was the Praxis
the Chinese do not define some crimes
as contradictory to the commonweal
until they've been objectified in practice.
Then the miscreant's retroactively in hazard,
a perhaps capricious billet
and often also fatal.
When they convict a malefactor
of capital offense on Tuesday morning
his ashes are in the mail
to next of kin by Tuesday afternoon.
The exemplary effect
of such expeditious justice
is possibly immoderate, but not without its uses.
Athenians tried it out on Socrates
for little more than sophistical adroitness.
Its employment back home
might make executives think twice
before peddling to the public
that more is less of anything,
especially ballistics.

Dangling Conversation

Li's a playwright but earns his keep
canting rimes and scoring
pratfalls for a local lowbrow opera troupe.
He says real theater's all but dead.
Buck up, I say, even Shakespeare had
his griefs. A star-crossed peal of ordinance

burnt The Globe from balcony to pit once,
announcing the entry of Henry VIII, the King—
Act I, scene iv of one bright opening night.
The Bard himself's best britches would have singed,
but that pragmatical Sir Francis Bacon
doused them with a pint of bottled ale.

Li nods and smiles, thinly. Red Guards, he says,
made lame old Lao She stand in foolscap hours on end.
They beat him senseless with props from his
own plays, then drowned him out in Taiping Lake.
This was what they called "re-education."
Now they say it was all a great mistake.

Peter Michelson

The History of Lao Shui's Eyes

She calls herself Romola,
I would honor her with Lao.
"Lao Tzu, Lao Kung but Lao Shui, no."
Lao is conferred on many others
some half her age and service,

and half of those are hacks.
She calls herself Romola,
Seven of The Eleven Years she spent in stir
being "re-educated" in the labor camps.
She laments the revolution fading

from the eyes of Chinese youth—
who lounge about in coffee shops
or simply play it cozy
with the iron bowl of rice.
She calls herself Romola,

a name she got from foreign books.
She wears it like a scarlet letter.
Her highbrow antecedents
made her suspect with the Party.
Now her children purge their genes

by working in the trades,
and balk at reading books.
She calls herself Romola
and wears it like a scarlet letter.
Seven years she spent in stir—

now residuary blood clots
are hammering her brain.
She laments the revolution fading
I would honor her with Lao
She demurs amid the drone ...

her children's distillating genes,
their sad asylum in the trades ...
You can see it in her eyes,
sometimes opaque as soapstone
then again precise as jade.

Peter Michelson

MÍNGTIĀN MEANS MAÑANA

Mine host the cadre heads the delegation.
They want to find out how we're doing.
Well, not quite—they feel obliged to *ask*.
As I offer tea, they do.
I pour, and itemize my discontents—
Today, like yesterday, the day before
and presumably tomorrow,
Tianjin is gray and cold and bleak.
All of which, excepting bleak perhaps,
must be considered ineptitudes of God
and not the PRC.
They smile at blasphemies.
Neither can I blame you
for this my second day of disability
from that embalming fluid you prize, Mao Tai,
despite the forethought malice of your multiple *Ganbei*.
This brings chuckles
and delicious looks of wickedness.
However, the facts are these—
My wife and kids have bronchial dysfunction
not to speak of fever,
the air is foul
the woodwork thick with soot
the toilet broke
no hot water for a bath
and our apartment has no heat!
Otherwise, apart from curtains
to keep in what there isn't, heat,
and out what there's a surplus of,
eyes attending the foreigners' privy indispositions,
we're doing pretty well ... more tea?

Mine host the cadre, smiling, nods
and, like the others sitting in his greatcoat, hat and gloves,
allows as how these rooms *are* "slightly cooler"
than those at the *Youyi Binguan* in Beijing,
than which—with their steamheat placebos—
he'd told me our rooms here
would be, I quote, *no better.*
Oh super subtle rhetorician,
these are no better *by at least*
the incremental speed of falling bodies—
Shall I demonstrate? According to the theory
your body and this cup of tea
shoved out that window should
arrive three stories down together.
If we time it I can tell you
how fast you'll both be falling when you hit.
He says we'll be here "temporarily."
Or perhaps, he smiles and sips, these are quarters we
"prefer"?
Prefer to what, the street?
Perhaps, then, there are others we'd prefer?
Some with heat, I say, wouldn't be remiss.
Ah yes, heat.
Perhaps, then, there are others we'd prefer?
Didn't he just say that?
Are there some with heat?
Unfortunately there are not.
But perhaps we'd like to *see* some others
with the heat we might perhaps prefer
in these other quarters
if there *were* available some others

Peter Michelson

which, unfortunately, there are not.
Thanks just the same, I say,
but it was idle curiosity killed the cat.
Ah yes, he smiles. He sees what I mean.

Mine host the cadre then confers.
His colleague smiles and nods,
stands up, removes one glove,
exhales a frosty exhalation.
He's the cadre of technology
who's going to fix the heat.
Excellent, I say, and stand.
I'm not quite clear whether in this case
I'm management or labor,
but I know enough to know you don't sit on your can
while the proletariat proceeds apace.
The cadre of technology fixes on
the radiator his expert gaze,
rocks forward on his toes.
He has in turn a colleague, with whom he now confers.
Hem, he says with sapience; the other answers, *Haw.*
He turns and speaks. Mine host translates—
he wants to know the problem!
The problem is, I say as level
as I'd give the time of day,
the goddam thing don't work.
I smile solidarity at the proletariat.
He receives this solemnly,
approaches the radiator,
extends his hand.
It doesn't freeze to the old cast iron.

He invites his colleague to share
this laying on of hands.
Hem! he says with vigor; the other answers *Haw!*
He turns, portentously pronouncing …
Mine host breaks out in smiles, it's fixed!
Fixed! Fixed? How the hell can it be *fixed!*
There's heat, he says, impeccable English
enveloped in his frosty breath.
I too lay on my hand; it also doesn't freeze.
Lurking somewhere in the radiator's bowels,
it's true, is water warm enough to be in liquid state.
Heat, I say, *heat,* the object is to serve the people heat—
Improve the quality of life, get it!
What language does this Mandarin manqué speak?
I screw my patience to the sticking point—
As the immortal Chairman Mao has said,
I say, desperately casting in my lot with dialectic,
the theory of the radiator
is coextensive with its practice....
In theory, *heat.* In practice, *heat.* In body, *heat.*
The cadre of technology has but fondled the radiator;
the point, however, is to change it!
I may as well be talking to my pet parakeet.
It suits mine grinning host to think
my tirade's just a paen in praise of heat.
Ah yes, mine host's nodding smile persists.
He confers again with the cadre of technology.
They smile in confirmation—the radiator's fixed.

And about the socialist plumbing, I say
as the delegation's heading for the door.

Peter Michelson

A flush is to the toilet
What radiance is to radiators—
its absence is negation,
a contradiction of evacuation,
whereas its presence would facilitate
the workings of my Foreign Expertise.
Comrades, a working toilet, *please!*
Ah, mine host the cadre says,
but perhaps it's been repaired.
Perhaps it has, *in fact* it's not.
True, a workman spent a day installing parts
no one of which, goddamit, fits another—
Remember, Comrades, what The Chairman says
of sterile theory without the praxis
to execute its art!
Mine host confers with the cadre of technology.
Míngtiān, the cadre says.
Lord help us, *míngtiān* means *mañana*.

Enroute to the Misty Peaks of Old Li Po

Dawn. Our train's been sidetracked
somewhere between Qungqing and Chengdu.
No water in the cars.
At the station hose I join the queue.
A hundred villagers
as if by immaculate conception appear.
APB ... APB
Foreigner abluting at the village station!
I wash my face and hands,
performance no better than routine.
I smile, they grin.
What's that they say ...
He's got a hairy belly ...
Is his navel filled with mold...?
I brush my teeth,
they zero in ...
He's got incisors ...
See, I told you, molars made of polished gold ...
Toothpaste's foaming at my lips—
Oh Mao, Confucius and Li Po
it's China's Civic Virtues Month,
and I don't know the protocol ...
those infamous "Three D's"
Dirtiness, Disorder and Discourtesy,
Am I about to commit all three?
Despoil the "Five Graces and Four Beauties"?
Defile "Civility"?
Indicate the absence of a "Noble Heart"?
Oh circumstance sharper than a pastor's fart!
With five score of the Chinese body politic
attending every move

Peter Michelson

should I expectorate or no?
Then, egalitarian and fraternal
on the ties beneath our car's *ce suo*,
a sign, a steaming mound of shit.
So what the hell, I spit.
The gallery breathes its Ohs and Ahs,
distinctly granting approbation
if not outright applause.
The engine gives a lurch,
the conductor hollers *Women Zouba*, Let's Go!
With a bow and grin I board—
for Chongqing then the Yangtze,
downriver to the misty peaks enshrouded
in the opalescent verses of Li Po.

The Chairman Premeditates His Yenan Talks on Literature and Art

       I

He would have been a scholar-poet   wandering
discalced and shirtless in the hills
as he once did   cavorting
like a heliotrope   until
the peasants hooted and
he lectured them the virtues of the sun.
Somewhere else he might have been.

His father used Confucius like a whip.
He learned the sage in self defense
and well enough to hate
the patriarchal voice.
He wouldn't peddle rice.
Or Buddha either, as his mother wished—
the usual progenic dialectics. He could have been
a kid from Bremmerhaven, Amsterdam, Detroit …

He would have been a scholar-poet   which
he could have been but wasn't   and
became instead an emperor
which he couldn't be but would become.
You might call it contradiction.

And now among these loess hills
their yellow dust
relentless in the northern Mongol wind …

Peter Michelson

The Chairman was himself arroyoed in
distracting contradiction.   Bored with Shaanxi
he slept late, remained aloof
one might say elite.

He might have been a scholar-poet
and like those *artistes du mal,*
Beardsley, Rimbaud, Mallarmé,
who had he known he'd despise,
he preferred the rapeseed oil lamplight
to the light of day.

In its oddly scarlet silver flicker   his mind
ignited like an ICBM   nocturnal calculations—
the eastern angle of the Rising Sun,
the slippery insinuations of his "ally" Chiang, the "Crocodile,"
contrivances to leap   in history's steeplechase.

And the Chairman courted destiny,
kinship with the Yellow Emperor whose
yellow tomb lay nearby   toward Xian.
He played the enigmatic sage
indulged occasional verse …
The future was as clear as Hegel's prose.

Meanwhile   he'd build its model in Yenan.
From where   at last descended
from the Mountain with portfolio
and even as the Rising Sun eclipsed the east
and the Crocodile thrashed along the Yangtze,
he saw the Palace waiting in Peking   its

red plum blossoms poised   their ancient banner
unfolding to the future like a poet's scroll.

    II

Yes   as he had known they would
the poets came   and with what strokes
to grace the fragile flower?

He would have been a scholar-poet   indulging
antique verse.   In the lamplight's flutter
taking up his brush   he contemplates the pleasure.
Does he call it contradiction   or is
poète manqué distinguished from the daily worker
in whose field   the Word
is equivalent alike   to sword and plow ...

His hand moves swiftly
the words impatient in the brush
We smiled on the thousand peaks, ten thousand rivers
The Wu Meng mountains rose and fell like rippling waves ...
No   he thinks   not *fragile*
neither fragile nor a *flower* nor even *grace* ...
We simply kept our two feet going
Through ten hundred thousand enemies peaks and chasms
we kept our two feet going   and now we're here
the revolution's inexorable   yes, machine.
He smiles at the word *machine*.

He would have been a scholar-poet   wandering
as now these poets wander in

Peter Michelson

but for the obligations of Hegelian history
and esplanades of circumstance.

He thinks the poets think
a revolution's mere revision of an epic verse
a landscape scroll languidly retouched
carefully considered
respectfully polite.

These Confucian echoes ring in spite.
He drops his brush and stands   his shadow
on the wall a shadow of   a Changsha fugitive
disguised in Hunan hills
exhorting peasants to   yes if need be   terror.

And the Hunan landlords   their daughters' ivory
boudoirs trampled by   the peasants' dirty feet. Too
god-damned bad. The landlord thought himself
a tiger   that the peasants wouldn't
pull his tail or kick his ass
They damn well will   and did. Reasonable men
oppressed will terrorize oppressors   yes.

He smiles and paces. He
would have been a scholar-poet   but
he gagged upon the   silken literacy
of landlords   and their vicious mincing manners.
Now peasants take the landlords in their calloused hands
and pop their heads like grapes—
The truth is in objective practice.

Poets can move on over   hip by haunch
or they too can lose their precious asses.

He thinks   they want   like Prince Po Yi
to contemplate beside a lake
as white as poppy blossoms
and exercise exquisite intuition   while
paradise pops out as slick
as maternal fruits of labor. By god
They know no more beginnings   than
They do of ends   and even less of what's between.

The would-be Manchu mandarin   says
Marx and Lenin are Heroic Individuals   O Truly Poets
he lisps   *like Homer Byron and Rodin!*
Good Buddha Confucius and Zen Zan
I'd rather talk atomic physics with   a Lolo tribesman!

Are Marx and Lenin
the Master Painter's limpid strokes
prefiguring some mystic scheme   No
they've neither beauty nor revelation   they're just
extremely *useful*   an agency
as is the arrow to the aim.
When Genghis Khan bent his bow at eagles
he was precise   and didn't volley arrows
witlessly in space   nor yet dandle them in praises—
O admirable arrow   how like to arrowness
O admirable arrow ...
and never shoot at all!

Peter Michelson

III

What then were the problems to be solved
precisely   fitting art into
the revolution's functional machine?

In Jiangxi   he'd not survived on odes.
There   as on the march   he learned indeed
if the cart in front turns over
let the cart behind beware.

First things first.
Adopt the proper standpoint   and adhere.

He paces to his chair   the lamplight sputters.
He takes his brush   the words are waiting
Don't say the pass has iron guards
Today we leap the summit
The greendark mountains like the sea
The dying sun like blood.

Good.   Adopt the standpoint   and adhere.
We leap the summit with the masses
and to them give praise
and learn from them   that unpruned trees
how quickly go to seed ...

He'd praise the masses then?   Yes, them.
And Wang ... or Li ... or Song ... ?
You mean the entity, the soul ...
He flings his brush across the desk,

it spatters on his verses.
Their god-damned precious egos—
If they were landlords
their holdings would be ten thousand li
and we'd know exactly what to do ...

This brush   it's made of hairs
here and here and here   and
to each hair a hundred atoms.
Its being is brush   Its soul is making strokes
and neither's realized
if each hair goes awry   according
to some quixotic private will.
We trim the brush to save its soul
he smiles   each single hair   expendable.

I could scarcely cross the Swamplands *once*
yet Chu Teh *three* times guided columns ...
I was then   the cadre pin   he smiles
and he   the turning wheel.

Our objective is to raise the people   yes, agreed.
Does that mean splendid egocentric
idyls spiraling incomprehensively in air?
Or satire's dagger   probing
people's boils or warts   or worse   thrust
hiltdeep into cadres' imagined peccadillos
with whatever flair?

Are we   the Party   not the axle, hub and spoke
essential to the wheel   and if

Peter Michelson

upon its going it gouges traces
on some naively palpitating faces…?
His orderly brings the day's dispatches.

Wang … and Li and Song … will have to wait—
what after all's the source,
the peoples' life itself   a mine
whose every rift is veined with ore.

He smiles. He's talking like a *poet* Ah
of course   the bourgeois view
those many delicate varieties of people
hybrid roses   a worthy culture coddles.
At any one historic moment
there are in fact just two   us and them
where are you?

As a student   when
he yet would be a scholar-poet
he was meticulously clean
and loathed the peasants' ragged backs
the ox dung on their feet.
Pigshit   he says now
the pretty bourgeois sty we wallowed in.

Good again.   Adopt the standpoint   and adhere.
Yet   though social life
is more rich by far   than art
the people still demand the latter   why?
And things reactionary wrong and sly

are often artful   the greater art   though prized
demeans the people   why?

He lights his cigarette from the lamp
and paces to the map
exhaling   on the Japanese positions.
The orderly is waiting. He takes his brush
and artlessly articulates decisions.

IV

Alone again   the Chairman strokes his brush
art   politics   a unity
of politics and art   as immanent
yet austere as life among the people.

So far so good.
But here's a source of   escalating muddle—
the transcendental rhapsodies
of disembodied human nature.   Heroic Individuals …
they may be rebels   but
they don't make revolutions.

The abiding fact is social class   you serve
the proletariat   or else the bourgeoisie.
There is no imagination
abstracted from the interests of   its caste.

Lampoon the peasant for the merchant   the merchant
for the Court   For both
you lyricise the loyal servant   or filial devotion,

Peter Michelson

Praise the grace of idleness for mandarins
of silks and scents for beauties
For scholars entwine your syllables
to insinuate hermetic mysteries   In short
successful art accommodates   the ruling classes.

Good.   But as always   there's rebuttal—
the source of love and art   they say   are one ...
The one the one the one, I say shit!
I've hung my hat
upon the guardians of Dharma
that's all for which they're fit.

Love's a product of objective practice
and routine circumstance.
*Oh   the comradely wine of love   they moan
is being diluted in Yenan ...*   As they well know
the Crocodile's cup slops over.
And they come here because our wine is *weak?*   No
and neither is it syrup.
Let them accommodate its taste
likewise the measure of its force.
Our purpose is to cultivate a native grape
not import an Epicure's distillation.

And comes the poet*ess* who chops our logic—
If the revolution is   for all mankind   she minces
how can its heart   that's us   *not manifest its love.*
Is there either love or hate
without its cause   or
any such all embracing passion

as this so-called   *love of man?* Not a chance.
"The same old story / love and glory ..." Piss!
Each class is with the others
inexorably clashing.

The starting point is always   practice—
We love the masses
because we share their struggle.
We don't love man
because we hate our enemies   and they are men
men who willfully oppress us.

Ruling classes liked to advocate it otherwise.
Many sages did the same.
Well, so much the worse for them
morality without a practice.
This abstract *love of man* is like
an embryonic calf   *potential*   and that
only when we've spat in hand
and done our job   eliminated classes.

And   for all of their Byronic prancing
these dandies don't understand dark forces.
Oh they play at dark and light   opposing   but
it's a game of chess   not dialectic.

A moonless night has not the dark of moon's eclipse ...
just as the Rising Sun   brings darkness
the Red Sun rising   if need be
on the Crocodile's back   dispels.
Strategy is more complex than tactics.

Peter Michelson

Do the masses have their   darknesses?
Yes   they've lived their lives in caves.
Our purpose is   to lead them *out*
not have them marvel at the   labyrinth,
indulge the twisted genius   that keeps them *in*.

But compromise   they wheedle   is the death of art.
Compromise!   we take the Crocodile to bed
and find that he's got uses.
The only death of art   is death.   Thus
art like life leaps the summit
with   and not without   the living masses.

Yet   though social life
is incomparably more rich than art
people still demand the latter.
Why?   a higher level?
a greater power, nearer some ideal?
All auxiliary.   Unless
it pushes   people into history
and history forward into life   art won't matter.

The truth is always   with us—
its avenue is time   and practice.
Self-indulgence is the evil force
transforming boulevards to mazes.
The test is in the knowledge of the moment.

We already understand the fundamental point—
kill the parasite   that sucks its life
from the inequity of classes.

All human nature   bears a certain stamp
the consequence of practice—
A revolution's not a dinner party.
Its power is in the barrel of a gun.
Our aim's kept sharp with hate
Love is what the ruling classes advocate.

II
When the Revolution Really

WHEN THE REVOLUTION REALLY

comes it will come
    in the dead of winter, while

        you're walking
    down Clark Street
to the Cosmopolitan State Bank.

      The wind will
    knock an old man
butt over teakettle, his

          cane and shopping bag
    go sprawling. You
              stop and help him up.

       You take his arm.
He will prefer
    to carry the shopping bag

        himself. You
    will walk with him
three blocks to his apartment house. He

    will fumble with his keys. He
will mumble that
        he can make it now. It

    will not occur to him
        to thank you.
Then you will go home rather

Peter Michelson

    than to the bank, because
you should conduct only so much business
        in a single day.

 Or maybe it will come
in a bus in the Loop
     in August

  a steaming August afternoon, and
an old lady, really old
      with a cane

    and a shopping bag, mumbling
  to herself like
old ladies do, an

     old lady will announce
like old ladies do that
     she wants off at Randolph, and

    she'll get up creaky
      and slow, very slow, and
she'll take a long long time

     getting off:
put the cane on the first step
   take careful hold

     of the rail, put
her right foot on
    the first step, slowly

  twisting her
ponderous old body, then
  the other foot on the step, the

  cane, then,
on the second step
  shift her grip

right foot, body turning, left foot,
  and the same thing
   all over again

  to the ground.
And the bus driver waits
   very patiently and

  we all sit very
patiently and
   we will say, and

  we will mean it, that
*there's an old lady
getting off the bus, she*

  *goes very slowly
because she's old
  and it's hot and*

  *she's tired and
anyway she's not in a hurry.*
  Neither are we. We're

Peter Michelson

> *just sitting here
> and it's all right. That's
>   the way old ladies do.*

> Then you'll know
>   the revolution's really ...

Parable for Our Time

A little bird whispers in their ear
and, inexplicably, the city hires
freaks and bums.
Music, dancing, jugglers, clowns, poets
carrying on at the city center.
Pretty soon people start hanging out there,
eating their lunch,
singing and dancing and carrying on,
climbing on the Picasso,
which is all right
because the engineers figure out
how many cubic inches of people
can fit on cubic inches of the Picasso
and they build it strong enough.
But there's a cop who doesn't know that
and he figures it's not OK
so he goes to tell everyone to get off.
Meanwhile, there's this girl who,
either as a tactical freak ploy
or maybe she always wanted to diddle a cop,
anyway she seduces him
before he tells everyone to get off,
so they hump happily in the shade of the Picasso
while everyone is singing and dancing and carrying on.
After while everybody goes home or back to work,
just sort of boppin along
bop bop bop …
The cop, who is so pleased he
forgets to mess anybody over,
goes home and tells his wife he got laid,
in the line of duty,

Peter Michelson

keeping the peace.
She says, *what!?*
He says he got laid.
So his wife says, *how was she?*
He says, *what?!*
How was she?
The cop is speechless.
So his wife says, *never mind, I'm better,*
and anyway you don't need to go to work to get laid.
So they put the kids to bed
and then they go to bed, and sure enough, *she's better!*
He never noticed.
So the next day he doesn't go to work.
He stays home and gets laid.
And the people are all getting together
at the center of the city, carrying on.
Singing, dancing, talking, laughing.
Climbing on the Picasso.
Each day the cop stays home and gets laid.
But he forgets to tell them down at the cop station,
so they keep sending him his check
because there's never any trouble on his beat.
And the Picasso is strong enough.
Even the bosses come down for the party.
The rest of the city is just like before,
but down at the center everything is fine.
Singing and dancing. Carrying on.
The city gives the cop a raise.
Everyone agrees he's earned it.

Variations on Shooting an Elephant

    a theme by Orwell

Surrealists have taken over. Completely.
Contradiction is the ultimate logic.
The answer was so simple. They couldn't believe
it. Except Salvador Dali could. He made
his money in advertising. Contradiction
is a lot more interesting than lies.

"The revolution's not gone well." So (lies?)
Juanita. Castro. I know completely
what she means. Call it contradiction.
Fascists have extravagance in logic
but they're boring. They won't win. We're made
better. People prefer the circus, believe

it or not. Shooting pachyderms we believe
in and are charmed by more than puffy lies.
No surrealist ever shot or made
dead elephants his trade. Though fascists have, completely.
(What's so boring in them is their logic)
Than they are more ultimate is contradiction.

In re: *because?*—of all the contradiction
(who knows?) people pay to see what they believe
in, shooting elephants: it's impossible to lie,
it's hit or miss. Unerring. Circus logic
is unboring. Contradiction. Surrealist completely
undercover. Wisely. People's made

Peter Michelson

by god! *perverse*. Elephants by some are made
to link their trunks to tails. Contradiction
is diverting but people's not completely
fooled, them on their (skirted) hind legs dancing. Believes
in, people, mostly ultimates not lies.
Shoot the pachyderm demands the people. Logic

bores them. Luckily? Their logic is the logic
of ice cream Wally says. He knows. They're made
better. (We're) Bored to death with lies.
*Give us geeks, fascist! Contradiction's
what we thrive for.* People most believe

what most they can't believe on. Surrealist completely.
Shoot, fascist! Impaled on contradiction
logic is what logic's made. Believe
what lies you will. Perform our will completely.

Earth Air Fire Water and

bingo a bayonet,
a set of gears ... We're free
to worship as we please

but nonetheless we also
celebrate our sweat.
"The first thing's

maintaining body heat."
We're free ... there
are signs enough—eagle

talons, sickles, bayonets—
we get the point. The gears
meanwhile are synchronized ...

things progress apace.
Easier and easier
does the wheel turn. We

keep our noses to it.
We don't double-clutch.
Earth air fire and water ...

a little pressure—
more bayonets, more gears ...
we mind our Ps and Qs ...

we get a teapot
that don't just whistle "Dixie."
Beneath the leafy chestnut

Peter Michelson

we mean business. We
keep the beat, attend
contingency … more

bayonets and gears,
more teapots … we whistle
while we work. Maintaining

body heat … we worship
as we please.

                Meanwhile, however,
this morning's clouds

glow as if the sun
were soul. And then the
mountainside ignites, the

bark of dormant oaks,
the prism in my window
fills the room with light, the

stainless sun attends
a ripening contingency,
moves on …

we don't get up
for work. The light's as mad
as starlings screeching *cat!*

We worship as we please
a miracle more
immense than Lazarus, than

steel ... we stand
like little boys blinking
in the sun,

without panache,
believable as teapots whistling ...
our blood is hot,

a brew so rich
we speak in tongues,
bearing intimations

more durable than
body heat or steel, more,
shall we say, like thistledown ...

Peter Michelson

Disarming

>   *for M. K.*

We will come stalking
but stalking as antelope do, in pairs—
our nostrils flared into the wind
our delicate veins pulsing
our soft eyes alert.
We will see you and know instinctively
you are dangerous.
We will lope to the far side
of this small valley....
Knowing you have mortars and
that your range is infinite,
we want to be centered
in the pure focus of your scope.
I will rest my head lightly
across the back of her neck.
You will remember horses shining
in a meadow when you were a child.
The rush of your pleasure
will be headier than the fragrance
of roses, more precise than
the fine crossed hairs of your exquisite sight.
You will see the unfathomable white
of our bellies, the richly mottled
dun of our backs, divinity
in our slender legs.
You cannot let us out of your sight—
you cannot help it
nor can we.
Poised here in this sheltered valley
within range of your full power

we are keeping faith.
You will remember this day.

You will remember ...
You will tell your children ...
You will bring them to this place
to the far side of the valley
where we stood among the mountain flowers .
They will twine them into wristlets
saying 'Yes yes ... I know ... you
saw some antelope ...'
The sun, in its orgy of conflagration,
will set beyond the ridge.
But long after, as it sets over San Francisco Bay
or Guam, these peaks will glow.
Neither the whimper of hungry kids
nor Coyote's dismal insinuations
can make you leave.
The patience of your faith, now,
is infinite. You have declined
prerogatives of fire and ice, explaining simply
that, yes, the sun *will* rise tomorrow
and the creatures graze as is their wont—
nostrils flared, delicate veins, vulnerable
white bellies alert
to fragrant dangers.
We cannot help it ...
as I nuzzle gently her nape
and the healing sage burgeons at our feet,
we are keeping faith
in the crossed hairs of your perfect sight.

Peter Michelson

Contemplating the State of the Art, The Lover Lies Back in the Dentist's Chair

The important thing is not this book of poems
or that asparagus but this *thing* call it ache
call it Froggy plucking his magic twanger

or Aphrodite the marrow of my bones but
it declines the gratification of being I mean
here or there to put your finger on

I mean I want to take hold I mean impossible
imperatives occupy the same space
at the same time not some cheerful vulgarity

or winsome figure, "my glistening swizzle stirred
her wet martini," or other evasions of
implosion I mean molecules not

as in some transcendental compactor but
exquisitely tactile after all I do
bury my face in her belly sucking the fragrant

skin deep into my nostrils yes but I
want to put myself in her skin looking
in investing every tissue and synapse

altogether obliterating whatever
isn't her sinew and soul sometimes I want
so much my brain is vestigial and my teeth ache.

Our Children's Feasts

I

in memoriam Inez

Though children call us father we are children
until the ones that we call father die.
And we would have it so, would keep dark
eventualities from our door.
Above the doorway horseshoes, or for feast
days sprigs of mistletoe. Palms perhaps.
But before the exodus an SOS.
And we would save the body too, splash sheepsblood
on the lintel, so grievous sometimes is
the working of great wills. Then too wandering
is nexus, hard imperative for finding
out our way. Its own imperative.
Therefore we travel deserts in the dark,
to find a place of laughter and of feasts
and keep the ghost within our body's scope.
In short, give thanks once more that we're arrived.
For we are eaters all, invoking what
we must. We find our gods within the model
of ourselves. And celebrate. Hoo Ha!
And we would have it so: to live forever
in our children's feasts, ghosts dancing
to the rhythm of our own laughter on
our graves. So, in time, give up the ghost
that, like smoke rising from our ashes,
we'd be breathed in our children's lungs,
their every breath a song, our celebration.
As the world made flesh initially

Peter Michelson

was respiration, mouth to mouth
and man to man. Such holy profaning
from the start our guide. And after supper
Jesus sang, the word made flesh making
words in time, raising with his sleepy
friends a song imbued with bread and wine.

II

for E. A. & S. G.

We place our fecund godling in the place
of feasts, this kitchen. He sits in the center of things.
Perched grandly in the manner of a man
with gout, this household god, the eater's model,
who knows the taste of things, awaits us. We
do not know him nor one another, yet
we have come from many lands, our dead
unburied past—its bones mulching in
the marrow of our own—pushing us
for generations (*is this the place? or this?*)
precisely to this room where we are met at last.
Our priapic idol greets us one by one.
He waves us in. *Muchachos,* he laughs, *Muchachas,*
begin! And much commotion attends expression of
his will. Bushels of salad mount and cheeses
grated on a board. Tortillas frying
at the stove. Refritos, chilis bubble
at the brim of dented, sooty pots
we eaters cannot but admire. Children
giggle at the door. Our godling orchestrates

all things in harmony with one will—
prepare the feast! We do. This kitchen is
omphalos, this gouty sage its nave.
We do as he says, the doing our reward.
Our children's mouths run over with chilis and wine …
their orisons of laughter, rising with
this room's rich smoke, sound praises through the spheres …
the air is lucid with hosanna and Pernod.

Peter Michelson

          All right, what
she was she was stoned. She
                wasn't—though it seemed

          she was, or
more accurately it seemed she was after,
     understandably enough, an

          idyll, but clearly
she wasn't happy. Still
     she spoke—was it anticipation

          or reminiscence?—she
spoke of smiles. And
               of an impulsive urge

          to be with him. But
naturally it came late. At the time
her decision, not to, seemed right. She

          had things—fences? bridges?—to
tend. And, as timing is
          everything (she had, inexplicably,

     first read in her manual, determined
not to be merely a woman, how
    to fix a broken timing

         gear), it was now
too late. Though he (however she
     defined him, for

>   even there she had
> choices) was not more than half
>   a mile away, she didn't know exactly
>
>   where. And by now—though
>   at the time her choice was
>   right—he
>
>   was perhaps on his way
> somewhere else. So
>   there were the old problems, time
>
>   and place. Still,
>   she spoke of smiles. And
> of discovering, stoned, the surprises
>
>   lurking in the
>   self. But: by herself? (That
>   after all was
>
>   what she wondered.) At
> the time her choice was right. Now
>   it was too late. He
>
>   was either someplace
>   she didn't know or
> on his way (whoever he was)
>
>   to someplace else. And
> she was, perhaps by choice (about
>   that too she

Peter Michelson

    wondered), alone. Grinning
at the couch, the space heater, the
  desk. She spoke, with some

    slight hysteria perhaps,
of smiles. And what she wondered, perhaps,
     was what the night

    portended. At the time
her choice was right. But
      now she was alone, grinning

    at things—her book, her
lamp, her shoe. All right, she
    was stoned, she

   wasn't though
it seemed she might be, happy. And
     she thought, perhaps too much,

   of smiles. Within half a mile
there were those to smile with. But
    she didn't know

    exactly where. And,
  even now, were they
on their way to someplace else?

from *Pacific Plainsong*
(1987)

I

Preface to *The Works* of H. H. Bancroft

Volume XXXI, *History of Washington, Idaho, and Montana, 1845–1889*, pp. vi and vii

There were those determined to
serve not (as Vancouver) by
stepping on shore to luncheon and
reciting (ceremonies) to the
winds, nor by naming the
great River of the West for
(as Robert Gray had done)
his ship. There
were those who
served (as they determined) by
possessing there were those determined
servers determined (while securing to
themselves such homes as they might
choose) who by possessing
(of the territory) chose
to serve by taking there
were those who (by possession) chose
securely there such homes as
those (determined) who declining
luncheon and some ceremonies, chose
to serve and did (their
government) by taking territory
and (ceremonies to the winds) they
served by actual occupation.

Peter Michelson

        I need not here repeat their
        narrative I need not here
      repeat those (bold) measures by
    which these men of destiny their
          destiny achieved. I
         wish only to declare they
     faced (those early pioneers) the
         mystery, they faced the
great unknown—though (by whimsy, by
     merest chance, or as we say
          it fell out that) they
    had found the choicest portions—
    they had (of the great unknown)
       found its fertile soil, its
     wonderful inland sea, safe
from storms, always open to navigation,
     abounding in fish, bordered
         many miles wide with
the most magnificent forests on earth.

     So (securing to themselves such
    homes as they might choose) it
        did (does) not require
       a poet's vision to picture
      a glowing future, albeit dim
       in the reaches of time. And
    to lay ever so humbly destiny's
cornerstone was worth the (humble)
      toil and privation (abounding
      in fish) the (safe from storms)
    danger and the isolation (always

open to navigation) for
to lay destiny's cornerstone
(even) ever so humbly is worth it and
there were (weren't there)
among them those determined to serve.

Yes, and (incidentally)
this inland sea with
treasures inexhaustible of
food for the world and
fifteen hundred miles of shore covered
with pine forests to the
water's edge and
surrounding it small valleys of
the richest soils, watered
by streams from pure
snows of the Cascade
and Coast ranges, half prairie and half
forest, warm sheltered from winds enticing
the weary pilgrim from the eastern side
of the continent to rest in
their calm solitudes, so well did
God (and those who were determined to) serve

(though it was true that
the native wild man
still inhabited these valleys and
roamed the mountains to the number of
thirty thousand, the
incomers were sons of sires who
had met and

Peter Michelson

        subdued the savage tribes of
                America as they
      pushed West from Plymouth Rock
         to the Missouri and beyond—
therefore they had now no hesitation).

              For bred to believe
      that British and Indians would
         melt before them they
(British and Indians melting before them)
         had no hesitation and
     (though there were among them
          native wild men) they
      (sons of savage sires) had
   no hesitation and (bred to believe
      in melting pots) they melted
       British and Indians before
         them and (determined
     to serve) enticed weary pilgrims
       to their calm solitudes for
   there were (calm, determined) those
        men of destiny facing
       the great unknown there
       were those bold those
determined who (securing to themselves
      such as they might) chose
        not (unrequired) a poet's
   imagination (the British and Indians
      melting) for among them were
      the sons of sires determined
    to serve and they (securing what

they chose) they had (picturing
a glowing future) they had therefore
(without ceremony) they had therefore now no hesitation.

The sources for this volume are those which have enabled me
to write all my volumes.

II

Today I met a rude, humble people ... scarcely better than animals ... the women busily engaged like swine, rooting up the beautiful verdant meadow in quest of wild onions ...
  —George Vancouver, 1792

... a *people,* yes, but rude
  & humble, scarcely better—in
fact in context—the equivalent of
    swine ... a rude &
  humble people, the equal of swine   animal
unclean ... *rude   rood* ME. AS. OFr. L. akin to Gk.
  ME. AS. OFr. L.
    akin to Gk. *rood* the dream
of the rood ... the passion
        buried, obscure ... the dream
  of the rude buried & obscure
barbarous or ignorant: as, *rude* savages
lacking refinement, culture, or elegance:
    as, *rude* savages ... harsh,
  discordant, not musical: as, *crude*
        ME. AS. OFr. L. akin
to Gk. bleeding, raw, akin to
        cruor blood
  congealed, thickened, bloody
akin to *cruel* ... disposed
      to inflict pain & suffering, to
    take delight therein: as,
they are insolent, uncivil, crude, cruel, rude
  scarcely better nee equal to
        swine ... they take delight therein

   ... a *people*, yes, but humble
      & rude ... crude & cruel
a relentless disregard for the rights & welfare
    of others ... the women
  like swine rooting
      the *verdant*
    meadows ... the women
  like swine rooting
      the *beautiful*
    meadows ... beautiful & verdant
these Meadow Manors these Meadowbrook Hills the
  women like swine discordant
  rooting Elysian Fields ... barbarous, bloody
    raw, congealed ... giving
    birth beside the trail ... bloody
      inelegant swine, these
    are The Great Chain's missing link
      to be forged
    with relentless regard or disregard ...
    the fire burns
insolent, uncivil, akin to L. akin to all
      we speak ... in or at one with
    neither grace nor generosity we are
the heirs of arrogance set sail
      with the gift of fire, with
    the advantage of Greek ...
     we take delight therein ...

     ... a *people*, yes, but rude
    & *humble humilis*
      akin to *humus* ... the soil

Peter Michelson

            the earth ... lowly
lacking refinement ... taking delight therein
      humus, humilis the soil, the earth:
                        as, a humble people
    rooting the earth, taking
                   delight therein ...

humus humilitas humanus humanitas
        akin to man akin
               to earth ... engaged
   like swine
              amid the verdant meadows
       amid abundant forests
         amid the navigable inland seas ...
humilitas humanitas humilitas   in
     quest of wild onions   I
met today a rude & humble people
    humanus humanitas humaine humayne
akin to *cruor* akin to blood akin to birth ... beside
       the trail, there
      was no wonder at the birth
                 or blood ...
Whom do you seek, O swine of the field?
   humus humilitas humanus humanitas
     the dream the dream of the
  dream of the rood the dream of the rood is
      buried deep ...
    akin to earth akin
        to man ... *cruor*   crude
cruor rude ME. AS. OFr. L. akin to Gk.
Whom, O swine of the field,

                    Whom do you seek?
         who placed us here is here ...
we come from no country ... and what we seek ...
                    the dream
                         of the rude ... *humilitas*   in quest
                    of wild onions ... *humanitas*   to
                                   take delight therein ...
a sow's ear in a silk purse
                         today I met a people
               The Great Chain's missing link
to forge   relentless
          regard or disregard: as
     at My Lai we are under orders
     certified sane
               in all respects ...
     humilitas   the fire burns
               humanitas   the fire burns
          sane
in all respects   regard or disregard
          relentless   Whom, O scarcely more
     than swine, do you seek?   O Whom
                    uncivil inelegant people ...
     humanitas humanitas humanitas
               ... we are here
               uncivil inelegant people
                    engaged like swine
rooting the beautiful meadow in quest of Whom
          O people ...
                    humilitas humilitas
               ... we are
     the heirs of arrogance set sail

Peter Michelson

                with the gift of fire, with
           the advantage of Greek ...
                    hybris hybris
                under orders
                        certified sane
            we take delight therein ...

III

Plainsong at Lapush

Locked in locked
in this (neither past nor
present) anachronistic village is
shrouded in its battered sea
spray air—its shoreline stacked
with stoney bleached enormous (two
feet thicker than
a man is tall) carcasses
of trees, their jagged roots upended
claw the (sullen) sky—all
all is shroud and bonewhite gleaming
along this brittle shore.

A (well past bearing) squaw
rocks amid the baskets she
no longer weaves and looks beyond the mist
bound shore complaining men no longer ride
the open boats or
risk rough water out at sea.
In the village (white) Mark
Westby teaches Indians (one or two) their
ancient craft of carving—offshore
Shell Oil blasts leviathan
and salmon, sounding lively
messages of profit through this pall
of spray. But I came to see
fishers at their trade, and
their past a curio,

Peter Michelson

              their present obsolete
           I watch the ghosts of Kwakiutl,
        oil-skinned and glistening, astride
              the pitch and swell, they
                work their dark pacific
sea and bend to haul up gleaming
              nets, to bring rich flesh
                of fish to air; their
             calloused fingers slap the
              gaff deep in the heaving
             gills they snare—implacably
they gaff that signal writhing, gaff
             and know an old despair.

IV

Leschi's Mad Song

(From Telstar) camera pans
whole of continental U.S., at
Seattle zooming to
intersection of Yesler Street (original skid
road) with Elliot Bay waterfront to
(chief) Leschi, then, wearing Brando/Zapata
expression of (profound)
ennui and dedication, standing at
corner—fish trucks, tourists, and
stevedores in background, as
Mac and Muff (teeny boppers) play
(discrete) grabass, watching jellyfish
orgasm in the bay. All is
tranquil and godfearing
bustle of enterprise when
Leschi (in war paint, headress, and bear's
tooth necklace) shakes
a tambourine and bellows, "White Mother
fuckers," then (having just the night
before seen Sammy Davis Jr. as a TV cavalry
sergeant) adds, Black Mother
fuckers!" All freeze agape (except Mac in slight
grimace as Muff, freezing, catches his
foreplay digit in sphincter
lock), Leschi begins war
dance, chanting Nisqually
medicine ("The times they are
achangin," punctuated at

Peter Michelson

grace notes with lyrical *White*
and/or *Black Muahfu*) and
prancing about intersection plunging
a harpoon through tires and
denting hoods and fenders with
tomahawk. All freeze until traffic cop comes
to and shouts "All right, Mac, cut it!"
(Mac, misunderstanding, looks up
terrified, frantically doubling
efforts at digitus
interruptus from rigid Muff), Leschi
ignoring cop continues his demonic
attack on Yesler and waterfront. The cop
unable to solicit help, as
all hold freeze, launches into "Indian
Love Call" which awakens Muff (much
to Mac's relief), who is
in real life a beautiful octoroon Nisqually
princess studying voice at Cornish
School and she (loving men in
uniform) responds with Kundry's seduction
aria from Parsifal" which
baffles cop until they get together in
duet of "God Bless America (and nobody
else.)" They exit (after encores) to
an emergency cop phone and call
the riot squad which
comes and pounds Leschi (who continues throughout:
chanting and prancing oddly about banging,
poking with tomahawk and harpoon until
subdued) to Burgerchef tenderized consistency, as

camera pans from business-as-usual at
Yesler and waterfront while the traffic cop is
locked with Muff in an inarresting sex
arrangement, as (close-up)
jellyfish undulate in bay.

Scene two opens in courtroom, as
prosecutor concludes, "... from every
lamppost, by the good Lord above we'll
have law and order in this
land." The jury goes
berserk, foreman grabs up a flag, others
produce fife and drum, all march and sing "Yankee
Doodle" around the courtroom. Spectators remain
calm though fuddled. As Public Defender
shrieks, "My client, even though a filthy, backward
savage, pleads not guilty, but
personally I wasn't at the scene of
the crime so
it's hard for me to say."
Jury starts up again but judge
gestures hypnotically with
outstretched palm. "What," he asks
Leschi, "have *you* to say?"
Leschi gestures hypnotically (gives
judge the finger) and shouts *White Mother
fucker;* sees a black cop, *Black Mother
fucker!* Cop keeps stonyphizz but
straightens smart black leather
cravat and adjusts smart black leather
ammo holster belt, resting

hand on revolver butt, eyes
smiling *Man it more blessed
to give (shit) than receive (it)—
every motherfucker for himself*
(sings "Ol' Man River").
Public Defender interjects to
(bug-eyed, outraged) judge
"My client means this
whole thing is mistaken, he's
just an actor studying his
role on the street, but
personally I wasn't at the scene of
the crime so
it's hard for me to say."

Pandemonium again, until
Prosecutor cries, "Objection, his
act's too good, Yesler Street's no
stage for pissant players to
bugger traffic while
they hone their mocking
methods ... We're witness here
to muckrakery and (reason)
treason spreading *seeds* throughout the land. I
call on witnesses to (lie)
testify: this bad good actor's stopped
up traffic ... *He whomped my hood, Dented
my truck, Was up to no
good, Why he said fuck!* Too
much! The judge leaps up shrieking, "If
niggers can by God learn not to

shit in corridors and keep
a tight zipper on their fly (black
cop covertly checks his) then
you stinking savages can learn to
live like Christians (jury
cheers, spectators, still calm and
fuddled, applaud) and (by God) you're GUILTY
GUILTY GUILTY and we'll (by
God) make you all good (dead)
injuns or know the (by God) reason
why" jury foreman leads "locomotive"
for Law and Order) as
(from Telstar) camera pans whole
of continental U.S. and
orchestra overlays muted "America
the Beautiful" on electronic reverberations of
Everett Dirksen reciting (in
unctuo) *with liberty and justice for all ...* as
Leschi goes to gallows
and "... on the 19th of
February the unhappy
savage,
ill and emaciated
from long confinement and
weary of a life which
for nearly three years had been
one
of strife
and misery, was
strangled
according to law."

Peter Michelson

        strangled according to law
         the law according to
          which he strangled
             was law
          (according to law)
         and he was strangled
      according to perhaps not his
             law
    but according to some (which?)
             law
        he was strangled and
          according(ly)
             he
           dangled
     from and jerked about (dares
      Justice jerk her lovers off)
        the gallows (?) That
       act's tough to follow, but
before "a large concourse of people (there) assembled"
      he (weary) according(ly)
        according to some
         perhaps not his
           law he
     (an emaciated method
     actor studying the lead
       for his own life
         story) was
          strangled
        according was
   strangled according to law.

Though few chiefs survived it and
"His (Leschi's) death may be said to
have been the closing act of
the war on Puget Sound,"
"Kissass (stet) Kussass, chief
of the Cowlitz, (lived)
114 years. He
was friendly, and a Catholic."

Peter Michelson

V

Seattle is described as a dignified and venerable personage, whose carriage reminded the western men of Senator Benton; but I doubt if the Missouri senator would have recognized himself... in this naked savage who conversed only in signs and grunts.

Sealth, your brazen
image labors now beneath the
bowels of pigeons, or
now and then a gull will
bring you tidbits from the
bay. Your molded eyeballs gaze
on produce of the land you've
vanished from—at this postcard skid
road square, at tourists, sailors, cops, sullen
Indians, and reeking Yesler
burns. Chief, my (suburban) youth was fed on
myths of your (pacific)
wisdom. Our ancestors loved you (we were
told) and named their town for
you. You weren't (like Kitsap) pushy or
(like Leschi) mad. You knew
your place. And (footnotes to your history say) you
taxed the settlers (shrewdly) for these restless
nights you walk, your ghost
unearthed by (chatty) invocations of
your name. That fraud vindicates a
savage (naked) born and remnant to
the Age of Reason. You
learned the game. History footnotes (at least) a man
who bites a dog or an injun who
screws a white man without

contracting clap. Counselor, even
though (poor bastard) you didn't have the
style of a (Missouri) senator, you
counselled well to keep your tribe from
war. The Dwamish fished
in peace, were dry and warm in
winter, and died a quiet
death. They
extinguished themselves with dignity. Knowing
your (civic) duty, you merchandised
your cosmos to these states. So
now I come to see your (memorial)
reward, to Yesler where your noble profile
sits, your
brazen headress gleaming
in the rain, and
your stern (prophetic) glare ignores
the shoulder (twitching) where
a balding eagle shits.

Nor mountain no
nor bronze nor
stone are monument
gargantuan howevermuch
enough

Though Crazy
Horse
emerge at last from South
Dakota hills, his
mountain-blasted tombstone's

Peter Michelson

        pork-barrel boondoggle
              DRAG
   show, (*See, folks, step up, look close—*
      beneath the Breechclout,
            stone)

    A concrete buffalo three
      stories high gazes
       down a North
     Dakota draw, hot
    for cows that never
        come
  gargantuan howeverrnuch
       enough.

     Air ripper, jack-
  hammer, blast, beam, and
     balls we shape
Mohammed in the mountain, lament and
  scan the edge of earth: such
   remembering—poem, plate, or
     song—is molding
    making all horizons take
     cadavered shape.

   Emerge at last though
     Crazy Horse he
may from South Dakota hills his
       ghost is
       friendly.
    (Him good injun)

Custer died for your sins
says redskin bumper wit.
But vestigial Sitting Bull, amused,
knows more precisely who wins,
how little the sea churns
or earth burns to pay for sins.
When Joseph, who survived White Bird Canyon,
Big Hole and Absaroka,
survived the treachery of Assiniboines and Crow,
was hounded thirteen hundred miles by Sherman's Army,
haunted by starvation, cold, spectres of extinction,
When Joseph sent to Sitting Bull for help
he (the Custer killer) said
Joe, do you, like Crazy Horse, expect some miracle from these hills?
You might as well piss upstream
to keep water from the dam—
give up, man,
Custer was a bad scene from a (B) flick—
but the ultimate (comedian) is Uncle Sam.
No matter how the sea churns
or earth burns to pay for sins
the guy that lasts is the one who wins.

In 1866 old Seattle watched
the sun, at Alki, extinguish, ripple orange, warm and
conjure sachems, their shimmer, his eyes, visions,
shimmer trails behind the sun—Seattle, tired
and prophetic in his impotence, saw old ghosts (no
ghosts) ghosts in '66. He learned
from Jesuits, and mad Leschi's execution, to
read graffiti on statehouse (outhouse) walls.

Peter Michelson

>   Nor mountain no
>   nor bronze nor
>   stone are monument
>   gargantuan howevermuch
>   enough

Seattle, this naked savage who conversed in signs and grunts, says to President Polk:

Day and night cannot live together. The red man has ever run before the white man, as morning mist before the morning sun. But your proposition seems fair. My people will accept the reservation. We will live apart in peace. The words of the white chief are the words of nature speaking to my people, speaking out of a dense darkness....

It matters little where we pass the remnant of our days—they will not be many. A few more moons, a few more winters ... tribe follows tribe, and nation nation like the waves of the sea—that is nature's order. Regret is useless. Your decay may be distant, but it will surely come. Even the white man whose God walked and talked with him as friend with friend cannot deny his destiny. We may be brothers after all. We shall see....

>   (this land is ours
>   or yours your ships your
>   cavalry confirm
>   the stars are sky is
>   dark our visions dark our
>   gods gone your
>   god grins your
>   cavalry your ships confirm
>   his grin it

matters little where
we pass our days your
guns diminish gods your grinning
cavalry confirms
it little matters I
shall not mourn I
shall forget my
god I
shall sign your deed this
land is my tribe is
blood this land is graves holy
ashes holy land is mine is
sacred ours
or yours
your cavalry your gods and dead
leave their land or graves wander
fields beyond the sun our
dead remain their dust is
rich with blood white
man the dead are bloody
dust white
man the dead are dust
dust prevails our
dust we bathe
bloody our visions white
man you will never be
alone be just
remember blood the
dust is not without its power.)

Peter Michelson

In the morning fog off Alki in the bay
Decatur's cannon prowls.
Dolphins arc before her dripping prow,
and from the sky
gulls crash clams against
the indifferent shore's rewarding stone.

Nor mountain no
nor bronze nor
all the elegies of man are
monument gargantuan howevermuch
enough

VII

Centenary Sequence for the Dreamers

1

About suffering they knew little more
than anybody else, the ancients
and old masters. Tragedy, said one,
is imitation. He was wrong.
Tragedy, as he like the other also
knew, is when you choose—or don't—to drink
the hemlock. And questions of art are, we say
these days all too unwittingly, questions
of execution. So, we find, are those
of life. Questions of art, then, are questions
of life—matters, that is, of execution.
And after suffering, no matter whose,
we would not be purged. They taught us wrong
those who sought the laws. Ask him who chose
the hemlock or him who told the tale.

2

Knowing depravity from Calvin
old Marc Whitman must have
died smiling, as a
jagged Cayuse hatchet jellied
his relentless brain.... One
hundred years prove
he didn't smile
in vain. This happy
valley reeks with God's
inexorable plan, his

Peter Michelson

grace: here
Whitman came with
Calvin's god and small-
pox malignantly in
hand; with Augustine's heart
burnt cork he smeared
alien stone
age souls, he
dipped their well
pocked bodies in this
valley's many waters—at
Walla Walla vestigial un-
elected savages atoned
grim souled Swiss or
rare Babylonian
sins …

Waiilatpu, place of
rye grass, once
ground for this
valley's native councils,
now it honors
Whitman, his
mission and his
kin. His hilltop
monument tapers to the
sky—a finger gesturing
abuse, enshrined, officiously
fenced in. Down
the hill, across
a road, beyond

> the mission's old
> foundations, a rutted creek
> bed commends the Nez Perce,
> Walla Walla and
> Cayuse, drained long
> since and dead ...

3

It is the soul of things the thing's soul
whatever it may be the soul of
we must discover. And can. There are
arguments in history worth hearing.
We do what we can, though some say *must* and others
will. Nonetheless, we do. And poetry
among them is not much. We may agree
on that. Yet, as the Dr. said, every
day we die for lack of what is found
there. True, the state of gods is not what
it was ... Likewise authority, and magicians
among us now are entertainers. Still
one quite lately says, "I am not
an entertainer," putting us on our mettle.
It is hard work for us, this talking ... like
heavy lifting it buzzes in our heads ...
too heavy lifting every day, said Yellow Wolf ...

Peter Michelson

4

Smoholla the Dreamer's Song

My young men shall never work
For men who work can never dream
My young men shall never work
For men who work can never dream
And wisdom comes to us in dreams
And wisdom comes to us in dreams

Sa'ghalee Tyee   Sa'ghalee Tyee
Show me what is in your heart
Show me what is in your heart
I will tell them all
I will tell them all about it

Sa'ghalee Tyee made the red man first
He made the red man first
The Chinaman who sews and irons
The Chinaman with a tail
The Chinaman who sews and irons
The Chinaman He made last
All the rest ... the Frenchman and the priest
The Boston men King George's men all the white men and the black
All the rest are in between
He made the red man first
They were called the people
They were called the people
And like the eagle He gave the red man wings

On these shores grew many people
And the strong oppressed the weak
Sa'ghalee was angry   He took away their wings
On these shores grew many people
And the strong oppressed the weak
Sa'ghalee was angry   He took away their wings
He said the lands were common   And the fishes in the sea
Sa'ghalee was angry
He said the lands were common   And the fishes in the sea

Sa'ghalee is the father and earth the mother of man
Yet the white man tells me *plow the ground*
Shall I take a knife and tear my mother's breast?
And the white man tells me *quarry stone*
Shall I dig beneath her skin for bones?
The white man tells me *make hay be rich* like him
How dare I cut and sell my mother's hair?
Sa'ghalee is the father and earth the mother of man
Sa'ghalee is angry   His people deny the law
Sa'ghalee is angry   He makes the white man strong
He does not love them those who sell their lands
He does not love them those who buy and sell the land

We freely take His gifts
As they are freely offered
And no more harm the earth
Than would an infant's fingers
Harm its mother's breast

But the white man cuts and tears   He scars our mother earth
The white man cuts and tears   He scars our mother earth

Peter Michelson

And calls this work his mission
His soul is hard with work
He calls this work his mission
And Doctor Whitman says we sin
His mission mutilates our mother
Bringing poison and disease
His mission kills our children
And his medicine is sin
But the white man tears the prairies
And the white man gouges forests
And mutilates the body of our mother
He drives stakes into her bosom
He marks it off in squares
And calls this work his mission
With work the white man's soul is hard
His mind diseased with sin

Sa'ghalee is angry and earth the mother of man
Sa'ghalee is angry
He said the lands were common
And the fishes in the sea
He will drive away the people
Excepting those who keep the law
He will drive away the people
Excepting those who keep the law

Come Sa'ghalee to the center here
where I live   in my heart
I set my feet upon this mother earth
I set my heart upon the great north star
That star ever in its place

I keep my heart upon that star

He will drive away the white man   back across the sea
He will drive away the white man   back across the sea
Our mother earth is slashed and torn
Sa'ghalee will make her new
The people and the creatures
Sa'ghalee will make her new
The people and the creatures
Sa'ghalee will make us new

As the left hand slides across the right
He will make the earth anew
As the left hand slides across the right
He will make the earth anew

The dead
The dead are coming
The dead are coming to sing with us
The dead are coming to smoke the salmon
The dead are coming and once again the buffalo
Our sons are coming to sing with us
Our daughters coming to dance with us
Our mothers coming to pray with us
Our fathers coming to beat the drums
My people are
Over the whole earth
My people are coming again
Over the whole earth my people are coming
Over the whole earth the red man and the law
The eagle tells me

Peter Michelson

The eagle tells me

And my young men shall never work
For men who work can never dream
And my young men shall never work
For men who work can never dream

5

Among us those who choose. As we step
up to the bar, the barkeep, resplendent in
his handlebar mustache, his sleeves bloused
by red silk garters, or sometimes sporting black
robes and judicial airs, the barkeep,
always affable and adroit, smiling
says, *All right, gents, name your poison.*
And smiling back, we choose. Graciously
we toss the man a tip. *Buy yourself
a drink,* we say. He deftly scoops the spinning
coin from midair and tests its purity
against his teeth. His teeth indent the soft
rich gold. Smiling, he pockets the coin. The truth
is this: *he doesn't drink,* he only pours ...
As if, said Joseph, *a man should come to me
and say, I like your horses, I want to buy them.
I say No, my horses suit me, I will
not sell. He goes to my neighbor and says, Joseph
has good horses ... I want to buy them but
he will not sell. My neighbor answers, Pay me
the money, and I will sell you Joseph's horses.*
Affable and adroit the barkeep changes
guise ... but, in whatever guise he goes
his sleeves are bloused for business. So, we choose.
And yet, we drink precisely what he pours.
Clever Lawyer, changes guise, and learns
to mix a drink.... *He was a man, as one
might say, of exquisite understanding, one
who was a Christian, one who learned the laws ...*

Peter Michelson

6

Is the story, then, too simple
for our own exquisite tastes? We
speak not here of noble
savages nor of their romance. This
story, though often told, has been projected
so transpicuous its plot must thicken
into mush. And it is after all
the lucid soul of things the
thing's soul whatever
it may be the soul of
we must discover. And can.
For matters of art, like life, are
matters of execution, and if
we would have the cause we
must go back. There
are arguments in history worth hearing …

•

We must go back, remember it?
as we were taught, Phoenicians
selling nuclear can-openers with Kabbalist
instructions coded into alphabet soup,
a free speed-reading course in every bowl,
remember it? the fruits of
enterprise …

•

And the grandeur? circuses, highways
and aquaducts still standing, laws,
Christians, and commerce spread like water
to all reaches of empire, the fasces

much admired still, and Christians
even then granting what's his (or yours)
to Caesar ...
                    •

And the glory, remember it? Athens, where
everyone, stripped to the waist, would work
the fields, keeping stoneyphizzed
at even *Dagmar's* tits, says Socrates,
swaying above the hoe, and
we all have upward mobility excepting
slaves of course, who are quite worthless, remember it?
the love of Truth, disinterested ... Socrates and
the barkeep discoursing, even as he drinks,
of Truth and State ... dying already in his belly
he is glad, this model citizen, to do his part,
as Athenians, said Pericles before the bier,
are yet more worthy since enlarging
their own inheritance into *empire*
extensively bequeathed to us their sons ...
                    •

If after suffering we would not be purged
we must go back, declining
ancient draughts and bromides
we vulgarians who came to conquer
and stayed to learn, remember it? as we were taught
the critics of it, Gibbon even, smug
and securely ... Mediterranean,
we must go back
            to?
            O Brave New World!

Peter Michelson

                Elizabeth and Isabella picking up the pieces
    of empire ...
               •

handing them to the fathers ... Adams, remember it?
praising Athens and Rome, *powers* he called them,
for having "honored our species
more than all the rest ..." Meanwhile
George Washington, throwing a silver dollar west
across the Potomac, winked and said, shrewdly,
"Stay out of foreign wars ..."
"By which he meant," said Quincy, a chip
off the old block any way you chisel,
"It seems the very will of *Providence*
that this entire continent be inhabited
by one people, but, since *Providence* (God wouldn't
melt in his empirical mouth) helps those
who help themselves, by all means stay
out of foreign wars ... let's
keep our eye on the ball ..."
    I have done nothing
    for their teaching, these
    savages, they will not
    listen and prate of the land
    our mission tithes from them ...
    and of the pox ...
    They are diseased
    and the hand of Providence
    removes them to give place
    to a people more worthy
    of this fertile country ...
So Spaulding, Whitman ... which? the barkeep

everywhere adroit conducts the Hallelujah
chorus, making the world safe for Providence
& Enterprise, Ltd., bigger
than the Hanseatic League Rothschilds Krupp or
Caesar himself Grandaddy to General
Motors the great neo-Platonic synthesis
of God and man
in a Rube Goldberg Whirlygig
raising Commerce from the muck
of its own jackboots
to sit with Him hip by haunch blowing
the very Will of Providence blood
rushing to His obelisk stone hard
with Destiny and Determination most
tremendous tool—opposable thumb and mathematics
notwithstanding—in the pornographic history
of the west. "And say what you will,"
said Buffalo Bill adjusting Joseph's bonnet
in the Hippodrome, "the Big Boy
sure knows how to use it ..."

•

Musical chairs, change metaphor, think
Levittown Shaker Heights Webster Grove Anaheim Louisiana
Purchase the Philippines
think *real estate*
the new world
suburb to ye olde
the ethos
laissez faire, remember it? bootstraps
opportunity keep your nose clean keep it
to the grindstone time

Peter Michelson

is money laissez faire, remember it?
as we were taught and made imago
Horatio Alger J. P. Morgan John Jacob Astor Howard Hughes (who
brought us suppliant and dripping in
their lobster grip Russian tuna disguised
as submarines *plus,* succulent
and dripping, Jane Russell's magnificent pout
and cleavage, for a roll in the hay
with Sergeant York and Lance Allworthy, "There,"
says the Voice of America, "*that* ought to hold
the little bastards," and it does it holds us
we love it absolutely
love it ...

       (this diatribe in fact brought to you
by a grant from Exxon simulcast with "Revelooshunairey Revels"
rock opera starring Marx Lenin
Trotsky Mao Castro and Sun Yat-sen, the
Castrati Chorale, brought to you uninterrupted
because
      there is nothing absolutely
      nothing to fear) so

precociously suburbanite are we
to an upbeat Mediterranean, our
future even now dependent
on the European Common Market, "What
you feared as the Yellow Peril," says Mao
truckin' with the Greek
generals, "you will come to know as the Yellow Sun
of your well being ..." we

must go back, the virus
as Burroughs said it would
is spreading ...

Peter Michelson

7

Dakotah Dreamsong

In Dakotah the Standing Bears the Kicking Birds
the Young-Men-Afraid-of-their-Horses lie down,
alone, where the great plains
slope to rivers—Big Horn, Musselshell, Missouri ...
And all around them
sky, sky and earth
and the creatures thereof ... they are one
with the eagle and the mouse
among the hip-high grasses, here
where the great plains slope to rivers
they lie down, alone, at dusk
beneath the Moon-of-the-Geese-Gathering ...

In the dreams they dream great
flights of geese wheel
in the morning light ... their breasts gleam,
flashing black and silver
signals from above the rising autumn sun ...
With each tremendous arcing turn,
like immense arrowheads in the sky,
from north and east and west, they come ... ghostly
silent apparitions drawn inexorably
to the living wheel, in the Month
of the Gathering of the Geese ...

When at last they wake
the young men wake to light
more splendid still
than aureoles of August moons, their
very act of waking, mediation,
so stunning is this canopy of arctic lights ...
They lie still, wide-eyed
beneath basilica more brilliant
than the galaxies ... Around them
neither owl nor coyote move,
caught by incandescence in
the arching ribs of rare Dakotah nights ...
Here, where great plains slope
to rivers, are young men more graced
than in their birth ... and wake
as if to silver geese auroral
in effulgent flight ... here
where waters of the river stop,
giving back upon itself the sight
young men purify themselves to see,
light and light and light
climbing the holy arch of night ...

Peter Michelson

8

"… as if a
completely new race of man were," Jonas
says, "emerging. Do you know what
The Byrds do with their money? They are
making huge signs and putting them along
the roadsides of California, and the signs
say one word: Love. That's where we stand
in 1966." Think about it.
Jonas says, consider The Byrds …
make roadsigns saying *Love*. Roadsigns. Love.
The Byrds. A completely new race emerging.
The Byrds. Make roadsigns love and money. Hmmmm …
Farmers need the rent. Foster and Kleiser
need the work. "Where are we *now*—the underground?"

•

This is exordium … this
is figura … exordium/figura … fine words, do
we know what they mean? We will know
whereof they speak … precisely. We are all tired
of fine words that come to nothing …
Exordium … Figura … Exordium Exordium Exordium
already it is taking shape
in our mouths … exordium
            we will know
            exordium
            we are all tired

•

the hands of Providence are diseased
and prate of mission

giving place
to a fertile pox
more worthy of these savages....
They are diseased, the hands
of Providence. Remove them.
Listen, they are diseased....

Peter Michelson

9

Joseph's Song

I am Hinmatoo Yahlatlat, *Joseph*, I
heard the thunder rolling I
counseled peace we
were as deer white
men the grizzly you
call me Joseph I
heard the thunder rolling (the
Earth is mother
of all and wisdom
comes in dreams) let
things remain white man
as they were made are
you white man the world's maker did
you make the sun? or
the grass to grow? as
well expect the rivers white
man to run backward as
that any man born free be otherwise
contented you
go where you please you
are not nor I
a child I am tired
of talk good
words that come to nothing Lawyer
Lawyer Lawyer white man there
has been too much

             talk by men who had
              no right to talk Hear
               me my chiefs if
           ever we owned our land we
               own it still the
            Earth is mother of all This
            I believe my people believe
              the same if *ever* ...
             we own it still as I
        am Hinmatoo Yahlatlat hereafter
         men may call me Joseph men
              may call me wise
            and brave and good but
              I am tired of war I
              counseled peace our
            chiefs are killed White
          Bird with Sitting Bull it's
                 cold we
           have no blankets children
              freeze my people in
         the hills my children dying Hear
           me I counseled peace Hear
          me my heart is sick Hear
           me white man as well
    expect the rivers running backward white
         man though you have won as
           well expect the rivers to
      run back as make a man contented
             who is not free Hear
       me white man as I hear you the
           Earth is mother of all Hear

Peter Michelson

                    me white
man as you move the mountains Earth
      white man is mother and
           wisdom comes
            in dreams it's
    cold our children cold our
      chiefs are dead Hear
me Hear me my chiefs from
where the sun now stands I
       will fight no more
forever Hinmatoo Yahlatlat
has spoken for his people

XII

Chiricahua Plainsong

1

Arizona Highways coordinate
    the landscape:
           even undulations help
    to make us
manageable.... tanks
rolling on rubber treads, like
    Buicks, there
and on the west side
        of Chicago ... "the
fiery forges of center earth
thrust up massive mountains, table lands
and anvil-like mesas. And
    with the powerful yet delicate tools
of creation—sun, wind, water
      and timeless age on
    timeless age—there evolved
a land of indescribable beauty ...
      while the Declaration
was being written and
        the war for independence
fought, Arizona
was a far-off nameless place ...
      Now, as then, a place
of peace and beauty."

Arizona Highways coordinate
    the landscape,

Peter Michelson

       and counties bear their names
      like tombstone plots
     coordinate with the delicate
   tools of fiery creation ... Mohave, Yuma,
     Maricopa, Yavapai, Pima, Pinal,
    Navajo, Apache, Cochise ... RIP.
Age on countless age
  of peace and beauty meld.... Like
     form & content, time
  & place, this melting pot, and
   willy-nilly we
are in a stew. Content
without form? No
   we are not prepared for that. From
     north and south and east
  the lost redeemers come—El Camino Real, the
     trail to Sante Fe ... Cortes
  & Kit Carson
blood & body of
     humid Mediterranean
  mysteries. Peace
on earth ... oil on troubled
    waters, not a ripple on
Lake Havasu, its smooth gleam
     silver beneath the London
  Bridge. Form
without content? No, we are not prepared ...
        So then,
Ponce, as guide to Arizona Highways
   in the sky, prone
  & languid on his pony, stroking,

                    indolent in
              the sun, when something
         caught his eye ...
                    "Apache! Apache!"
*Feet small, pony no shoes, Apache horse go all around
         just like Apache.... By*
this we understood Americans   in contrast
                    ride straight on
              from hill to hill. And

   so does Howard. If
war was hell and hell was hot
he came bringing heaven to the desert, peacefully—
         one-armed, unarmed on
      a bright bad day, one of many, at
                    Tularosa or
              the Bosque Redondo.
         Coordinate: intersect
      the Chiricahuas ... straight ahead
              from hill to hill.... I'd
   give my arm
to be the Moses of
         the Negro, he
said. And did. His
         mission next was Indians. That
      Christian soldier stuff is all right in its
              place, but
         he needn't put on airs
      among ourselves.... He
does all his good in such queer ways.... Missus
              the knees are wore

                   out every pair of pants I got,
                            prayin.... But

                when invited he did so, dancing thus—
          on either side a
    chatty Chiricahua woman held,
                       one to his left hand, the
                    other to his empty sleeve.... Form?
           Content? What
                       signs are these? A
                bit of cracker or sugar lump
          seduced Apache children ... they
nestled at my feet and
                    laid their little heads upon ...
                what signs? And if
    Cochise's son should learn to write his name?
                       Form without content?
             Our young women will attend to your lieutenant....
                And these, he said,
                    these are signs of war?

                                2
            Unarmed, deliberate as
    the destiny whose agency he is,
                                Howard
                         reins up before the monolithic
                Chiricahuas. Anxious
             Sladen whispers in his ear. The
                    Christian soldier
                 ponders face to face

the sacrificial: oneself,
one's faithful friend.... "Whoesoever, Captain,
will save his life shall lose it, but
whosoever will lose his life
for my sake
the same shall save it."
Form & content bemused
by paradox, Sladen shuts his yap.

Generals Crook, Miles, and Terry are
Spartan, big boned & bare knuckled
obedient servants to the oldest most
efficient forms
of truth. Nonetheless   there are
Cochise, Nana, Geronimo, names
children use today to conjure derring-do. So,
the mission is
change coordinates, intersect
Athens, Chiricahua, Calvary ... "By
God's help in Christ we
can raise men to the Beautiful and Good...." Form
& content, content
& form intersect ... Athens
Chiricahua, Calvary ... old soldiers
ponder sacrificial form ... the
old, efficient truths are
met in kind,
chin to chin, or not. And
even Grant
called the simple slaughter (of
disarmed Maricopas) simple

slaughter. Insoluble, form & content.
         Old Soldiers
              find such stuff
                 distasteful, a black eye
                              for the trade. So,
     change coordinates. Exterminating
angels deplore violence. It's
        inhumane. Deliver Negroes
                from their bondage, savages from sin.
                Civilities. Stick 'em bleed 'em
                pop 'em in the pot ...
                melt 'em meld 'em formaldehyde
                their thought.... change
      coordinates, form, and
                          content....   Paradox
                  is the art of speaking
                         with your tongue in both
                         cheeks (whose? hmmm, only
              Moses has seen God's hinder
        parts and
                only God can make a tree
                fall in the forest today.... form?
content?) at the same time. By
        which I mean we
                had to *destroy* the village
                                 in order to save it. Left
             to themselves Apaches don't
      have the sense God gave a flea, to
                         eat three meals a day. Even Pedro
                  who acquired manners quickly speared
                bread by fork and

                    took his meat with fingers. Form
                                and content ... Teach you
                        all I know and still you don't know
                                        nothing. But,
            when sober, Indians
        may be managed. And
by Christ we can manage even these ...

            Still, as soldiers go, he
    was one who had the / kind of guts it takes to
dance beneath a Chiricahua
                moon. Moreover, sugar lumps
        seduced the shyness of Apache children. They
                nestled at my feet ... they
            lay their little heads upon my
                    blanket ... Cochise's son
        learned from me to write his name ... the
                conduct of the women was
                        uniformly good ... I
                    introduced a system of
                        three meals a day ... the
    object of my mission was
            accomplished ... strange ceremonies
for consulting spirits were observed, the
        women's muffled moaning
                low in imitation of
                    the wind ... Cochise
                in mournful recitatif ...
            which side the Styx ... their
superstitions we did not know ... Cochise
                    in mournful recitatif ...

Peter Michelson

        he raised his eyes
     I observed his courtesy
        his simple grace
       his mournful recitatif
shi-cowah shi-cowah shi-cowah
      These mountains / are my home

3

    Wary, high among the craggy
        Chiricahuas, deliberate as
an old ancestral king Cochise
sees destiny approach disarmed, straight on
       from hill to hill. *Buenos Días, Señor,*
Though he kills ten whites for
      each Apache, still
from somewhere beyond the sea beyond
    the dawn there are whole continents indefatigable,
producing men with guns who wait implacably
   to wade ashore. *Buenos Días, Señor* ... may
     the son of god and light everlasting
upon whose empire the sun declines to set
       grab you by your scruffy neck and
shove you up the ass of buffalo or antelope
    or eagle and sublimate your form, give us
        something to believe in.
      Meanwhile, Señor, I
   do not want to go to Tularosa.
The flies there eat the horses' eyes.
Buenos Días, Señor. I have drunk these waters
and they have cooled me. I

do not want to go to Tularosa. He
holds his hard, lean hands before him.
   Buenos Días. Another race. Another
      time. His face is tinted
with vermilion. His hair is straight
      and black, streaked with silver threads.
         Destiny observes the silver threads
         and smiles. Destiny's a friend
      of time. *Buenos Días.* Cochise's shoulders
      sag. His courtesy. His simple
         grace. His wrath. Beside
      the point. Form without content. *Buenos
         Días.* To raid the Mexicans. To
      raid the gringos. Form without
content. *Buenos Días, Señor.* Apaches
beg indifferent skies, *come down, come down!*
      Buenos Días, Señor. Apaches
   want to die. They carry their lives
upon their fingernails. *Buenos Días.* I
   do not want to go to Tularosa.
      Buenos Días. I
do not want to go to Tularosa. The
   flies there eat the horses' eyes. *Buenos
   Días.* I do not want to go
to Tularosa. I have drunk these
waters and they have cooled me. *Buenos
      Días.* I do not want
   to go to Tularosa. I have
         drunk these waters *Buenos Días* his
courtesy his simple grace beside the point … his
         wrath   form without his courtesy

Peter Michelson

      his simple grace pondering

the sacrificial   the wind in the eagle's
     wing the wind among the silky
tassels of the small corn the wind
in my daughter's hair the morning
star above the desert   the evening star
    above the peaks the laughter
at the blossoming of cactus fruit the
     laughter in the cactus liquor the
       laughter in the morning songs the
      dancing of the virgins on the sunbeams the
laughter in the evening songs the
    dancing of the virgins on
the long bow behind the rain the
laughter in the mountains with
    the slender rain the young girls
singing in the third dawn when
the people fall in love there singing
      with the rainbow bright before me
      with the rainbow bright behind me
      with the rainbow bright above me
      with the rainbow bright below me
with the rainbow everywhere around me
      may I walk among the mists
of the long bow behind the rain
     being as it used to be
   and bounty in the dark clouds
   and ripe fruit in the baskets
     and ripe fruit bringing rain
and thunder rolling in the mountains

and when he talked to me my breath became
    form without wrath pondering the sacrificial
        his courtesy his simple grace his
      courtesy his simple grace his courtesy
          Buenos Días Buenos Días Buenos Días
          shi-cowah shi-cowah
      These mountains are my home …

Peter Michelson

XIII

"Bestride the Mighty and Heretofore Deemed Endless Missouri": An Essay on the Corps of Discovery

1

On the eastern slope
some were brazen, bold
as brass—the
young squaws even occasionally
hustling a ride in the strange up-river
sailing ship (a curious custom with the Sioux
and as well the Pawnee, they
give handsome squaws to those whom they wish to
show some acknowledgment. The
Sioux we got clear of
without taking their squaws.
They followed us two days.
They persist in their civilities....)

> But once past the Divide things were different. The Shoshoni women who had no word for white man but *tab-ba-bone*, enemy, were as if prophetically afraid. Coming within 30 paces unexpectedly of three female savages, they appeared much alarmed but saw we were too near for them to escape by flight. They therefore seated themselves on the ground holding down their heads as if reconciled to die.

Sunburnt, Lewis looked to be her natural enemy, but
when he stripped his shirt, showing
his white belly she appeared, he said,
instantly reconciled.

For the instant, as he took the old woman
by the hand and raised her up
gave her beads, moccasin awls, pewter mirrors and
painted her cheeks with vermilion, which
with this nation is a sign of peace, she
was no doubt for the instant,
as he said, reconciled. Now more than ever,
though she appeared otherwise to Lewis and
perhaps herself, she
was reconciled to die.

Her men, though armed and expecting enemies, the
Minnetarees, were disarmed by these pale apparitions
bearing gifts. Embracing
fate affectionately, in their way, they
place the left arm on our right shoulder
clasping our back while
they apply their left cheek to ours, saying
ah-hi-e, ah-hi-e.
I am much pleased.
I am much rejoiced.

Then the ceremony of the pipe
the sacred pledge of friendship, barefoot,
vulnerable and exposed, honoring
three times from East to North the points of the heavens—
the stem to the earth
then to the white men
then one another. Making
as only the women seemed to know
their peace with death.... "Several of the old

Peter Michelson

women were crying and imploring the Great Spirit
to protect their warriors, as if they
were going to inevitable destruction."

The Corps of Discovery came in peace.
They came with blue beads.
And scarlet red vermilion.

> On the western slope of the Bitteroots, as they approached the first Nez Perce village, most of the women fled to the neighboring woods with their children, a circumstance he had not expected as Captain Clark had previously been with them and informed them of our pacific intentions. The men seemed but little concerned and several came out to meet them, unarmed.

> Later, as if some aboriginal players devised the scene, Broken Arm took flour from the roots of cows and thickened the soup in the kettles of all his people, inviting those who would abide by the council to come and eat and those who would not should abstain. All but one, an old man, celebrate the feast.

And outside the lodge
the women, he said, cried, wrung their hands, and
tore their hair. The women, he noted,
filled the air with lamentations. The women
with their heads bowed to receive death.
The women riding with their children to the hills.
The women
always the women
filling the air with lamentation. What,
in their fear, in their womanly weakness, in

their women's hearts, what did they know
that he, Lewis, meticulously
noted their fear and lamentation?

> He told the chief, Cameahwait, he was sorry for their lack of trust. He told the chief that among white men it was considered disgraceful to lie, to entrap an enemy by falsehood ...

>> (There were yet he hoped some Shoshoni
>> not afraid to die. Or have you all, he said,
>> the hearts of women, and noted
>> again meticulously
>> that he had "touched the right string."

>> No, the chief said, I am not afraid to die.
>> The solemnity of the pipe, then.
>> And the women imploring the Great Spirit
>> as if, he noted, they were going
>> to inevitable destruction ...

> *Exultingly he thanked his God that he had lived to bestride the mighty and heretofore deemed endless Missouri.*

2

York
the big black buck
"servant" Clark said
the way a Virginia gentleman don't say *slave* or *nigger*
don't say *shit* if he had a mouthful.

Peter Michelson

    Said, "canoes of skins passed down from the two villages and many came to view us all day, much astonished at my black servant who did not lose the opportunity [my italics] of displaying his powers, strength &c. This nation never saw a black man before."

May be—can't say—they
never either saw a "servant" before.
Better they get used to it.
Going to see it a lot.
Going to be it. Soon enough
going to be more big
bad black curly-haired bozos in Dakota
than Pawnees.

Those aborigines much astonished at my servant indeed!
York carrying on with his powers and all,
not missing the opportunity. *He*
ain't getting no medals, large *or* small size,
picture of Jefferson.... All
flocked around and examined him
from his nappy burr head to his two-toned
pink and black toes. *He* don't miss
no tricks.... carried on the joke, he said,
and made himself more terrible
than we wished him to do. Yeah,
old York coming down *bad* right there at the start.
Don't miss a trick, putting them
Pawnees on. A little show,
black boy doing honest-to-god *black face*
right there on the prairie—heart of America .
Just, God knows, a little bit

badder than we wished. But OK
a little divertisement
in the middle of the big play.

Break out the fiddle now,
show them shuck footed Pawnees some *rhythm*.
He ordered his black servant
to dance, which (naturally)
amused the crowd
much, and even somewhat astonished them
that so large a man should be active &c.
Those people are much pleased with my black servant.
And he don't miss a trick,
showing off his powers ...

(and their women, fond of caressing ...)
old York must of had himself a time, their
women very fond of caressing
caressing I dare say
his powers, and
his powers getting bigger by the minute
making himself more terrible than
we wished and
you can make book on it too.
Old Stepnfetchit
being *baaad* right out there beyond the frontier,
just laffin and showing off his powers ...

    (there once was a Pawnee maid
    who said she wasn't afraid
    to lay on her back

>   in a prairie shack
>   and let a *black* cowboy!?
>   diddle in her crack.
>   And then to her surprise
>   her belly began to rise ...)

Ohhh Yassuh, Yassuh the dancer said
and then for prophecy
he ate her. Marsa Clahk, he
winks and says, you think *that's* fun,
you just waits til later.

> *What history records is that he made himself more terrible than we wished.*

3

Courageous, resourceful, and enterprising they had, Jefferson knew, "the true qualifications." Though lacking "a perfect knowledge" of botany, natural history, morality, mineralogy, and astronomy, they were in the end therefore found to be more reliable, American. More importantly, they were soldiers, men of skill and discretion in the use of arms—muskets of startling accuracy, the swivel gun, menacing, solid, authority unequivocally in its sweeping range.

And, though imperfect, they were men of their time, scientific—observant, pragmatic, detached ... enabling them to record flora, fauna, topography and native customs without prejudice (those people, Clark noted, are dirty, kind, poor, and extravagant, possessing national pride, not beggarly, receive what is given with great pleasure, live in warm houses, large, octagonal, forming a cone at the top left open for the smoke to pass, covered with earth on poles—willows and grass prevent the earth passing through. Those people express an inclination to be at peace with all nations.

Meanwhile, we tried the prisoner Newman last night by nine of his peers. They "did sentence him 75 lashes and disbanded from the party." The punishment of this day alarmed the chief very much. He cried aloud, or affected to cry. I explained the cause of the punishment and the necessity for it. He also thought examples were necessary, and he himself had made them by death. His nation never whipped even their children, from their birth.

(Note: the Arikaras are not fond of spiritous liquors, nor do they appear to be fond of receiving any or thankful for it. They say we are not friends or we would not give them what makes them fools. Those people express an inclination to be at peace with all nations.)

Also, they were practical and canny in matters of defense, enabling them to succeed where others failed—knowing only too well that *the treachery of the aborigines of America and the too great confidence of our countrymen in their sincerity and friendship has caused the destruction of many hundreds of us.* Those people express an inclination to be at peace with all nations.

Then too they were men exemplary not only in their skills but also in their morals, inspiring loyalty and discipline in the field. On Christmas Eve a Clatsop chief offered a woman to each of them, which they declined accepting of, and displeased the whole party very much, the female part, especially. This was the same party which had communicated the venereal to several of our party in November last. I therefore gave the men a particular charge with respect to them, which they promised me to observe. Old Dlashelwilt and his women still remain, but I believe, notwithstanding every effort of their winning graces, the men have preserved their constancy to the vow of celibacy which they made on this occasion to Captain Clark and myself.

No wonder, then, that they should fulfill their president's charge—to ascend the Missouri to its source, to cross the Highlands, to locate and follow the best waterway from thence to the Pacific Ocean, to establish friendly contact with the aborigines, to assert thereupon the power of the White Father over their trade, comfort, and well being, to make vocabularies of native languages, to make maps, chart geography, collect horticultural, botanical, zoological, and anthropological specimens, and "as indeed they did" make way for a prosperous commerce.

Courageous, resourceful, and enterprising, they knew, meticulously and instinctively, how to touch the right strings. Though lacking a perfect knowledge, they were in the end found therefore to be more reliable, American. The fruit of America. American. Those people always expressed an inclination to be at peace with all nations.

4

From the beginning they
were received with curiosity, and
nothing more whetted interest in their mission than
an exhibit of musketry and cannon. Which

they did regularly and with great effect. Always
of course advising that
the new White Father in Washington, he
who had bought them from the anarchists
of France, he who had bought them from the
monarchists of Spain, he
the White Father
who brought them the Word, he
desired to live and trade in peace with the aborigines.
And he, they said with what sense of irony we
do not know, he desired that
they live with one another so.

(Look back, they told Little Crow, the
Mandan war chief, with
what sense of irony we do not know, look
back at the number of nations who have been destroyed by war.
Reflect, they said, on what you are about to do.
If he wished the happiness of his nation he
would be at peace with all. By
that, by being at peace, and
having plenty of goods, and a free intercourse with
those defenseless nations, they
would get, on easy terms, a
greater number of horses ... if
he went to war, he
would displease his Great Father, and
would not receive that protection and care, as
other nations who listened to his word.
Happiness, horses, easy terms, *they said.*
Listen to his word.)

Peter Michelson

Among the Mandan they thought it well to aid and assist them against their enemies, particularly those who came in opposition to their councils. If the Sioux were coming to attack, to collect the warriors and meet them. The chief said the village was very thankful for the fatherly protection, that the village had been crying all the night and day for the death of the brave young man who fell, but now they would wipe away their tears and cry no more.

Rejoice, they said.
Listen to his word.

Among the Wallawallas several diseased persons requesting medical aid, to all of which we administered, much to the gratification of those poor wretches. We gave them eye-water. *It would, Clark said, render them more essential service than any other article we had it in our power to bestow.* A little before sunset the Chymnappos joined the Wallawallas and formed a half circle around our camp, where they waited very patiently to see our party dance. The fiddle was played and the men amused themselves with dancing about an hour. They were much pleased at the dancing of our men. I ordered my black servant to dance, which amused the crowd very much, and somewhat astonished them that so large a man should be active &c. They then requested the Indians to dance, which they very cheerfully complied with. They continued until ten at night. Accordingly took leave of these friendly, honest people.

Among the Nez Perce, a reception more equivocal. Here too we dispensed eyewash and liniment, gaining for our medicine, as Clark said, an exalted opinion (in our present situation, I think it pardonable to continue this deception.... *We take care to give them no article which can possibly injure them.*)

At dinner however
an Indian fellow very impertinently threw
a poor, half starved puppy nearly
into my plate by way of
derision for our eating dogs, and
laughed very heartily at his impertinence. I
was so provoked at his insolence that
I caught the puppy and threw it
with great violence at him and
struck him in the breast and face, seized
my tomahawk and
showed him by signs, if he repeated his insolence
I would tomahawk him ...

> *(thereafter, he—Lewis—notes*
> *the suggestions of an old man who*
> *observed to the natives that*
> *he thought we were bad men and*
> *had come, most probably,*
> *in order to kill them ...*

So, as all the principal chiefs were present, they thought it advisable to enter more minutely into the views of our government, its plans for the natives of this western continent, its intention of establishing trading houses for their relief, its wish to restore peace and harmony, above all the strength, power, and wealth of our nation, their well being at the disposal of its will, &c. Then, they amused themselves with demonstrating the power of magnetism,

Peter Michelson

    the spyglass, compass, watch, air gun, and sundry other articles
    equally novel and incomprehensible to the savages.

        (still, in his journal, the
        record of what the old man thought and said,
        that we were bad men and had come, most
        probably, in order to kill …

    After we had eaten a few roots, we spoke to them and gave each a
    medal of the small size with the likeness of Mr. Jefferson, and to
    some the sowing medals struck in the presidency of Washington.
    We explained to them the design and importance of medals in
    the estimation of whites, and as well the red men who had been
    taught their value.

        (still, in his journal, the old man …

The Nez Perce held a council on the morning of the 18th.
They resolved to listen to his word.
Then Broken Arm, the chief, took
flour from the roots of cows and
thickened the soup in the kettles of all his people.
He made a harangue, impressing
the need for unanimity….
Happiness, horses, and easy terms.
They listened to his word.

Meanwhile he—Lewis—scrupulously
reported, outside the lodge the women
cried, wrung their hands, and tore their hair, as
if, he said, they

were going to inevitable destruction.
And the old man
the old man said we were bad men, bad
men who had come, most
probably, to kill.... *And the women, he
recorded, cried
and tore, he said, their hair.*

5

Having himself lived to watch
McNeal straddle the creek and
thank his God that he had lived to
bestride the mighty and heretofore deemed endless
Missouri, he—Lewis—noted, the
evening of August 18, that
he had this day completed his thirty-first
year. (He
        spent the day in commerce, bartering a uniform
        coat, a pair of leggings, a few handkerchiefs,
        three knives and some other small things "the
        whole of which did not cost more than about $20
        in the United States" for three "very good
        horses" from the Shoshoni.)

Having, though he did not know it,
completed about half of his expedition and
nearly all of his life, he
conceived that he had "in
all human probability now existed
about half the period which I am to

Peter Michelson

remain in this sublunary world." As
always, in consciousness and style, he
was a man of his age and did not, like McNeal,
thank his God but spoke grandly of
sublunary contrition. He
reflected that he had as yet done
but little, very little, to
further the happiness of the human race, or
to advance the information of
succeeding generations. But,
as yet a man of his rotarian age, he
dismissed that gloomy past and
resolved in future to redouble his exertions
and at least endeavor to promote those two
primary objects of human existence—to
live *for mankind,* as
he had heretofore lived *for himself.*
A man of his age.
On occasion grand and grandly spoken.
On occasion gloomy and alone,
pacing, while others sailed, the shore.
Alone of that resourceful, courageous, and
enterprising band, the
fruit of destiny's own breed,
Lewis alone of those
recorded the women and the old man.
Lewis, the moody, the solitary,
perhaps four years later the suicide.

An old Nez Perce man, he said,
who thought they were bad men and

had come, most probably, in order to kill.
And the women, who cried
and wrung, he said, their hands and
tore, he said, their hair.
Lewis alone recorded the women and the old man.

Lewis, who made the savages sensible
of their dependence on the will of our government for
every species of merchandise as
well for their defense and comfort.
Lewis, who took care to give the children
of the White Father no article which
could possibly injure them. Lewis,
who dispensed medals of large and small size.
Lewis, who with his medicine, his weapons, his
audacity, his ambition, his genius incarnated
the spirit and power of his country ... this
same Lewis remarks the old man's prophecy and
that the women wailed.
Did he reflect, for all
that he advanced the information of succeeding
generations, did he reflect on his
resolve to live for mankind, did he, four
years later at Grinder's Stand on the Natchez
Trace, did he, reflecting, know
as he morosely squeezed the trigger
finger of his always disciplined hand, did
he know, remembering his trek through the savage
sublunary world, did he know,
remembering the women and the old man, did he,
at the fulcrum of past and future,

Peter Michelson

scanning as a haunted man dark horizons in
that dark night, did he
see and seeing know, whoever
triggered his long night dying, did he
know precisely, having traveled to its far edge
and back, did he know, as
he cut his biography in half, did
he know precisely why and what he, reliable
American that he was, had done?

*The Corps of Discovery came in peace
bearing the word, blue beads,
and scarlet red vermilion.*

6

For that we were no scholars
and lacking a perfect knowledge we
were found to be more reliable, American.
We followed absolute as mortal man can do
our high command. And
we came, as the old man said,
crudely calculating probabilities, as
the old man said and Lewis strangely noted,
we, the fathers of our sons, the
sons of our fathers, were
bad men and we came, most probably, to kill.

For coming without knowledge of what we did
we were bad men. For
pacifying the Nez Perce with eyewash, liniment, and

laudanum we were bad men.
For thinking we came in peace we
were bad men. For bringing Virginia manners
to the Nez Perce we were bad men.
For our courage we were bad men.
For our strength we were bad men.
For failing to know the probability of our being
bad men we were bad men. For
bringing the badness of men to our fellow man
in the service of our country
we were bad men. We
were bad men, as the old man said, bad
men who came, *knowing well that the treachery
of the aborigines of America and
the too great confidence of our
countrymen in their sincerity and friendship has
caused the destruction of many hundreds of us,* and
we came, by any historical calculations, we
came most probably, whatever we supposed, we
came, as our leader's journal remains
to remind us, we came most probably in
order and well prepared to kill.

Accordingly, we took our leave
of these friendly, honest people.

Notes

A few words about the section of new poems entitled "Mixed Frequencies East and West" are appropriate. The poems in part three of this section all derived from my time as a volunteer for Peace Brigades International (PBI), an NGO, in Colombo and a curriculum advisor for Eastern University in Batticaloa, Sri Lanka. When I followed my wife there in 1992 the civil war between the Tamil Tigers and the Sri Lankan government (symbolized as a Lion) had been fifteen or more years in progress. It finally ended with the defeat of the Tigers in 1992. PBI volunteers were from New Zealand, Canada, Holland, the United States, and Germany. We were tasked primarily with conspicuously tracking human rights observances. The premise was that a conspicuous foreign presence had a generally benevolent effect.

The PBI team lived collectively in a house in a working class Colombo neighborhood. It had been the home of an assassinated Sri Lankan politician, a not infrequent event. Ostensibly Sri Lanka was a government of both Sinhalese majority and Tamil minority peoples, but the reality was rather more complex and often enough puzzling. The team had a variety of functions, witnessing labor strikes, elections, talking with politicians, businessmen and other civil figures, presenting ourselves at court cases involving human rights, etc. Civil dynamics in Sri Lanka at that time involved a wide range of political, religious, ethnic, linguistic, and military perspectives—the war signaled the Sinhalese and Tamils as principal antagonists, in addition to which was a third entity of violent quasi-legal Sinhalese nationalists known as the Janathā Vimukthi Peramuṇa (People's Liberation Front), or JVP. Cheek by jowl with wartime enmity was the religious edginess between Sinhalese Buddhists and Tamil Hindus. This was complicated by minority Christians (both Roman Catholic and Protestant) and Muslims. All this was suffused by the aura lingering from Portuguese, Dutch, and British colonialism, leaving English to coexist as a semi-official "national" language just subordinate to Sinhalese and Tamil.

Life in Sri Lanka's east, where Batticaloa, known as Batti, is located, was considerably more rural and also features several of the famous Buddhist shrines—such as Polonnaruwa and Anuradhapura along with roadside Hindu shrines and a largish mosque at Kattankudi. But at any given time the countryside could be a war zone, as the Sinhalese army occupied areas that the Tamil Tigers contested as it suited their purposes. So, apart from occasional firefights, one was subject to two different civic, though not necessarily civil, authorities as well as unpredictable Muslim reprisals for Tiger attacks on the Tamil-speaking Muslims. Batti was a schizophrenic environment. On the one hand there was a normal life in which the various political, military, religious, and ethnic populations went about their daily doings; on the other there were the curfews, checkpoints, and ongoing threats of attacks from Tigers, civilian Hindus, Muslim Home Guards, and hostile maneuvers of the Sinhalese army. Batti, a Tamil town of perhaps 75,000 at the time, had a tradition of a kind of Tamil *joie de vivre,* considerably diminished by the war but still sufficiently alive that it wrestled buoyantly with the daily tensions, griefs, and uncertainties.

Notes to Selected Poems

"The Chairman Premeditates His Yenan Talks on Literature and Art"

The Yenan forum was held in 1942. At that time and until Japan's surrender in 1945 Japan was theoretically the common enemy of Chiang Kai-shek's Nationalist forces and Mao Zedong's Communist forces. Though they were nominally allies, Chiang on several occasions ambushed or otherwise sabotaged Mao's armies. During WWII Japan billed itself as the "Land of the Rising Sun." Though Mao was a poet (his poems are available in translation) he did not so regard himself in a practicing sense and used classical styles that he discouraged for contemporary poets. Though artists and writers had by the 1980s begun to wrest some relief from the strictures Mao laid down at Yenan, they continued to be the official artistic guidelines. The two lines "*We smiled on ...*" are verses by Mao. Zen Zan was a Tang dynasty poet Mao admired; he was a friend of the more famous Tu Fu. The "would-be Manchu mandarin" refers to Xiao Jun, a Manchurian writer subsequently put to labor in a coal mine and denounced in rectification campaigns of 1948 and 1957. "*Don't say ...*" is a quatrain by Mao. A *li* is about a third of a mile. Chu Teh was the principal general of the Red Army; Mao refers to an episode of the Long March. "*The comradely wine of love ...*" is a criticism by Xiao Jun. The "poet*ess*" is Ding Ling, in fact a novelist and frequent critic of Chinese Communist Party attitudes; she was denounced in several rectification campaigns and sent to labor in the "countryside" during the Cultural Revolution; she was released in 1978 and made several public speaking tours, including one in 1982 to the United States and Canada, but was then pretty much in alignment with Party policy.

from *Pacific Plainsong I–XIII*

From the preface to the first edition (1987): "From where the sun now stands," Chief Joseph said a hundred years ago, "I will fight no more forever." I would not redeem myself in Joseph's eloquence. Still, we have invoked ourselves in voices more remote by far. I do not, however, want

Peter Michelson

it thought that this poem, *Pacific Plainsong*, laments injustice to the Indians. Still less that it should presume to speak for them. It speaks, in whatever frequency of stolen voices, of the moral logic endemic to our history with ourselves. "We may be brothers after all," said Chief Seattle, "We shall see."

Acknowledgments

Grateful acknowledgment to the following journals and anthologies, in which some of these poems initially appeared, occasionally in differing versions: *Another Chicago Magazine, Chicago Review, Choice, Cincinnati Poetry Review, Exquisite Corpse, The New Poetry Anthology, The New Republic, New Orleans Review, Notre Dame Review, Poetry North, Prairie Schooner, Sniper Logic, Spoon River Poetry Review, Tattered Fetlock, TriQuarterly.*

About the Author

PETER MICHELSON's personae are poet, essayist, teacher and critic. In those capacities his work has appeared in a variety of political and literary journals and anthologies, including *An Americas Anthology, The Art of Friction, Chicago Review, Exquisite Corpse, The Nation, The New Republic, Notre Dame Review, TriQuarterly* and others. He has published six books, three volumes of poetry—*The Eater* (1972), *Pacific Plainsong I-XIII* (1978, 1987), *When the Revolution Really* (1984); two of critical prose, *The Aesthetics of Pornography* (1971), *Speaking the Unspeakable* (1993); and a critical edition, *The Extant Poetry and Prose of Max Michelson* (2000). He has edited *The Chicago Review*, and co-edited *Rolling Stock* with Ed and Jenny Dorn, and has been a Contributing Editor to *TriQuarterly* and *Another Chicago Magazine.*

In the 1980s and 1990s it was his good fortune to travel, lecture and write on American literature in China, India and Sri Lanka. Poetry from that time is included here in both New and Selected Poetry. In the early '80s, following the fallout from China's "Great Proletarian Cultural Revolution," he taught in Tianjian, traveled throughout China, and sent translations of and reports on contemporary Chinese literature to *Rolling Stock* and other American journals. During the civil war in Sri Lanka between the Tamil Tigers and the Sinhalese government he volunteered with Peace Brigades International, an NGO human rights organization, and was a consultant to Eastern University's transition from Tamil to English as the language of instruction. Eastern University is located in Batticaloa, which could in those years at times become a free-fire zone. India was rather more pacific, but its vastness and its many languages and cultural counterpoints offered their own complications as he traveled the subcontinent interviewing writers and introducing the work of Indian poets to American literary magazines. During 2001–02 he was a Fulbright Lecturer on American literature at the Abo Akademi University and the Turku Yliopisto [University] in Turku, and Helsinki University in Finland.

He is Professor Emeritus of English and Creative Writing at the University of Colorado, Boulder. He studied in Seattle, Walla Walla, Laramie and Chicago and lived most of his life, apart from travels

Peter Michelson

noted above, in the American west. He has taught at Jamestown College [North Dakota], the University of Wyoming, Roosevelt University, Northwestern University and the University of Notre Dame. He lives in Boulder, Colorado.

www.ingramcontent.com/pod-product-compliance
Lightning Source LLC
Chambersburg PA
CBHW030136170426
43199CB00008B/81